AN HONORABLE RUN

MATT McCUE

ISBN: 1-4392-3328-4
ISBN-13: 9781439233283

Visit www.anhonorablerun.com to order additional copies.

TABLE OF CONTENTS

PROLOGUE

1. The 2005 Mount SAC Relays 10k. *Part 1:* April 2005

In the misty chill of the night, the nation's best collegiate distance runners flocked to a barren dirt-red track in Walnut, California, a suburb on the edge of downtown Los Angeles. Under the electric lights, every skeletal runner chased one goal—to run a fast time. Forty-five degrees, no wind, elite competition, and a rock-hard track made it a godsend of an April night for those looking to light a blaze with their ropy legs.

I was there. I was fit.

Anxious, yet quiet, I sat by myself and stretched on a cold grass field next to the track, waiting for my 10,000-meter race at the Mount San Antonio College Relays. Before stuffing my black and gold Colorado warm-ups into my gym bag and heading to the starting line for a set of snappy strides, I paused to pull out a photo. The picture captured a pack of runners in action in the foreground. In the background, on top of the wooden bleachers, one man stood cheering. The only person in his row, his hands were thrust skyward, his energy focused on someone in the lead pack. I stole a look before tucking the print back into my bag.

Lined up three rows deep, runners crowded the start of the eighty-man field. Expecting a victory was unrealistic, but I hoped to dip under thirty minutes, an achievement that would add my name to the record book of University of Colorado running legends. A rewarding end to my tireless journey, the feat required six consecutive sub five-minute miles, a tough task even for those in shape.

The gun fired at 10 p.m. sharp. A tangle of arms and legs burst forward in unison as the leaders quickly distanced themselves from me. I settled on the inside rail—less confusion, less risk of being spiked or tripped. A college senior, I had grown accustomed to racing sandwiched amid the helter-skelter. What I had never gotten used to was finishing mid-pack; that unwillingness to settle was what drove me every time. Pacing myself during the early stages, I conserved my energy. At twenty-five laps, the 10,000 meters felt like the race of endless circles. It was a test of patience, followed by destruction. At the halfway point, I began my charge, driving my legs as hard as they would go for as long as I could manage. Hopefully, all the way to the finish...

Hitting my final lap, I drew comfort from a quote inscribed on my faded yellow Regina High School cross country T-shirt. "If you think you're dead—you're not." I felt dead, but the pain reverberating through my stomach and lungs reminded me that I was very much alive. I sprinted past the finish line and spotted the scoreboard clock: 29:33. Wow, an unbelievably fast time—four minutes, forty-five seconds per mile! I had done it! An official directed me to lane two, away from the lapped runners who still had 400 meters to go. My spikes accidentally dug into the rubber surface, and I nearly tripped over my own feet. I didn't care. I was beaming. The tightness gripping my shoulders slowly melted away and satisfaction replaced my pre-race anxiety. I snatched it up eagerly, unwilling to relinquish a single jot.

Gathering my gym bag, I looked for my parents in the bleachers, nearly deserted at that late hour. I had to celebrate with them before I could see Coach Wetmore. A man of few words and fewer compliments, I knew he would have kept one aside especially for me that night…

The journey epigraphs: three men, two paths, one story

2. Endo in the public library!

To fully understand a man, we must learn about his journey. It is there that we can find the pulse of his life. Some men prefer to keep their past to themselves. Ironically, they often have the best stories to tell. I'd place Mark Wetmore squarely in that category. He reveled in being an enigma. If there was one thing that could give him life, however, it was running. After I graduated from the University of Colorado in May 2005, I asked my former coach about his odyssey. His answers struck a chord in me. His motivation reminded me of my own.

A native of Bernardsville, New Jersey, Wetmore had arrived in Boulder, Colorado, in late August 1991. Thirty-nine years old, he had no friends, no job, and no particular idea of what he would do for money. He was fond of quipping that if he couldn't find work, he would make a decent living as a burglar. He had been to Boulder in the past and knew it was a town with potential, equipped with the best public library in America. He hoped to coach long distance runners.

Upon arrival out west, he sought out a running trail, one that would be steep and hilly, empty and unpaved, as it crept through the mountains. Studying a topographic map carefully, he found what he was looking for twenty minutes outside of Boulder. He parked beside the green five-mile marker of Magnolia Road, where the elevation touched 9,000 feet. Stepping out onto dirt softer than the concrete he had pounded back in Jersey, he started running west. He ran down a little hill with a vast meadow on the left. In the long grass surrounding a small pond was a herd of elk that had

left the woods to quench their thirst. Mark Wetmore took it in:
the elk, the pond, the small log cabin at the far end of the meadow
with its weathered gray fence posts, and the towering peaks of the
Continental Divide, still shouldered with snow fields, against a
backdrop of brilliant blue sky. He had discovered paradise.

That day, he forged a lifelong friendship with Magnolia, a rutted, lost-in-the-mountains, off-the-beaten-track, windy dirt road,
overrun with kamikaze drivers who lived in the woods and raced
their 4 x 4s and Subarus within inches of anyone who ran there.
But when the maniac drivers weren't around, Magnolia Road offered a quiet refuge, perfect for his long runs, that allowed him to
cover up to twenty miles. What was he training for? Nothing. He
simply ran because he had to.

Larry, Mark Wetmore's mentor from back home, reinforced
his decision to stay in Boulder. "It's October and it's still seventy
degrees?" Larry would tell him over the phone. "You're a genius!
What a move! Ten bookstores? I'm on my way! They have Endo in
the public library? Brilliant! Don't move an inch!"

Wetmore listened. He staked his tent at a campsite until he
found a room to rent a week later. Boulder quickly became his adopted home. Greatness would soon follow.

3. The station wagon with blue vinyl interior

In contrast, Bob Brown's journey ended where it had begun:
in Iowa. A diehard Hawkeye fan, Bob had spent all but two of his
sixty-five years within the flatland state best known for producing
great corn and great wrestlers. In Iowa City, Bob lived with his wife,
Darlene, who used to be his high school sweetheart, and their four
children. He drove his widowed mother Vivian, who lived close by,
to pancake breakfasts after Sunday Mass.

Brown had never intended to become a running coach. A high school basketball player, he had started coaching to spend more time with his athletic children. In Iowa City, he had worked in the recreational therapy department at the University of Iowa hospital, never deviating from the chosen path of mentoring young people that he had embarked on years ago following graduation from college, first in inner-city Detroit where he oversaw the youth programs at a recreational center, then in Independence, Iowa, at the Mental Health Institute.

In the summer of 1987, Brown, then forty-five, returned to his alma mater, Iowa City Regina High School, and shared his simple idea with the school's athletic director who was also his brother-in-law. "I'd like to start a cross country team," Bob said.

The AD stared at him blankly. "This is football country!" he deadpanned. "I'm not sure you could even field a running team. In this school, the boys play football."

Bob didn't give up. "The kids who don't play football need a sport during the fall," he persisted. "Please, let me try."

The AD agreed to his proposal. A station wagon whose interior was covered in blue vinyl transported the inaugural team—five boys and two girls, along with Coach Brown. Iowa City Regina, a small 1A Catholic high school with an enrollment of 250 students, had a cross country "team"—the girls didn't have the minimum of four athletes to field a complete squad.

In their first meet, the boys' team finished last. But over the next seventeen years, the team would grow from humble beginnings and establish its own traditions. Championships would be won, legends would be honored, and those kids who needed a sport to complete their lives would find a friend and mentor in the small-town coach who lived his life inspired by the simple motto: "Nothing but my best."

4. Run fast

Both Mark Wetmore and Bob Brown were driven by a simple passion: they loved coaching runners. Every year, they would bid goodbye to seniors and welcome incoming freshmen. While their teams changed, these two unique forces would remain constant, living the convictions they preached. I was the other factor, common to both. The eager runner, I barreled down the fast lane, connecting—and colliding—with each coach along the way.

Born and raised in Iowa City, I had driven the same eight-mile route to Regina, eaten the same cafeteria food, and followed the same shirt-tucked-in dress code all through my twelve years in school. A Regina "lifer", I had attended elementary, middle, and high school in one building, traveling through the grades with nearly the same sixty classmates. Our mascot was no lion, tiger or other ferocious beast. It was a blue and yellow crown, creatively named "Crownie".

At the beginning of my senior year, I wanted nothing more than to leave Iowa and head to college where I planned to pursue my dream: running fast. It sounded simple enough. Unfortunately, not a single college coach had recruited me. That complicated the matter somewhat. But it didn't deter me. When my alarm clock buzzed at five-thirty in the morning, I never peeked blearily at the darkness outside before going right back to sleep. I sprang out of bed. And I ran. Without fail.

Our family of six lived in the country where the desolate roads offered a prime training ground. I claimed the role of the hunter and hardened myself to accept the prospect of toiling through the miles alone, targeting anyone who slept in later than I as a weak bit of prey.

Coach Brown, the wizened veteran who had turned his home-made program into a source of envy for Iowa high school coaches, seemed like the perfect match for me. When I joined his team as a freshman, he guided me with the wisdom and patience of a father of four, placing me on the four-year plan to state championship success. Eager to win right away and often, I put myself on the one-year plan. That was only the beginning of our differences.

Built sturdy and strong like a football player, Coach Brown would invite the entire team to stand with him at half-court during our school pep assemblies. He spoke patiently, preferring not to talk about the team's state championship banners hanging above. Instead, he focused on his runners' work ethic and positive attitude. His quiet voice and unassuming tone had a certain power, capable of holding the student body's attention in the minutes prior to dismissal. "Everyone on our team is important," he would declare with a grin, "because without the people in the back, no one would be there to push the team forward."

As a senior, I finally realized there was more to life than winning the Iowa state championship. There were collegiate national championships too. While Brown contentedly drove our team bus to rural communities with multiple town names like Clear Creek Amana, I was hooked on Chris Lear's *Running with the Buffaloes*, a day-by-day account of the University of Colorado's 1998 cross country season. At a college best known for skiing and partying, the Colorado runners fully invested themselves by, among other things, going to bed at ten on Saturday nights. Their objective was to rest for their eight a.m. Sunday-morning long runs on a devilishly strenuous road, whose sole comforting aspect was its innocuous name: *Magnolia.*

The more I read, the more I convinced myself that I needed to join the most dominant herd in the land—the Buffaloes. This competitive culture that held such powerful appeal for me could be attributed to one man alone: Coach Mark Wetmore—a guru, a mystic, a genius. I knew little about him other than the fact that he lived in the mountains, had a ponytail, and ran every day. He had logged at least two miles every day for nearly thirty years. He had coached runners, including club and high school teams, for almost as long. From 1988 to1991, he had been the head distance coach at Seton Hall. Then he had picked up and moved to Boulder, joining the Colorado cross country team in 1992 as a volunteer assistant. Three seasons later, he was put in charge. In the next eight years, using Magnolia Road as his cornerstone, he would coach two NCAA national championship teams, twelve NCAA individual champions, and dozens of All-Americans. Coach Wetmore's results spoke for themselves.

What intrigued me most was how every year, he granted a few blue-collar workhorses the privilege to "walk on". A handful of walk-ons, athletes not on scholarship, had qualified for the national championship team and earned All-American accolades. The dim possibility of achieving similar success acted like a powerful magnet for me. Wetmore's words made me nearly salivate with enthusiasm. In *Running with the Buffaloes*, he had told his team, "Look, this is what I am…I don't play golf. I don't have many hobbies. I don't have a wife. The bottom line is: I'm here to make you guys run fast. When I go to sleep at night, my mind's churning, thinking of ways to make you guys run fast…"

I. PACE YOURSELF!

The Early Years

I. The time trial: spring 1995

Long before I had heard of Mark Wetmore or knew about Bob Brown, I was like every other thirteen-year-old; I found running for the sake of running mind-numbingly boring. However, during the spring of seventh grade, I followed my friends going out for track and field and signed up for Regina's junior high team. I hoped to run the sprints—the shortest races offered.

On the first day of practice, the team walked to the expansive athletic grounds behind school for the 400-meter time trial that would determine the team's sprinters. Since I played football and basketball, I figured I was in good shape and that running in circles couldn't be too hard. My confidence wavered right before the trial, when I saw my teammates lacing up track spikes like Olympians. Each second-hand pair sported either a hot pink or purple Nike swoosh. Standing in clunky trainers, I silently begrudged my mother for her refusal to drive me across town to buy a pair of flimsy footwear.

Even lightweight shoes wouldn't have saved me. Four teammates made up the staggered start on me before the first turn. I watched them effortlessly lift their legs and glide away down the backstretch, their sheer gracefulness a taunt. Digging deep and gritting my teeth through the lung burn, I tried to catch them in the homestretch. It didn't work. I finished closer to the back of the pack than the front.

The next day, Mrs. Potts, my track coach and English teacher, assigned me to the mile, the ultimate last choice of anyone my age. I was crushed. Yet, the sobering experience might have been one of the best things that had ever happened to me. Humbled, I would emerge a new person.

Though it would not be my first defeat, the time trial unexpectedly triggered a moment of awareness. I wanted to win, and, for the first time, confronted the truth: my natural ability would only take me so far. It was, evidently, not far enough. There was only one solution: hard work. I vowed to rise at dawn when my competitors slept in, greet the rain when they stayed indoors, and keep going after they had given up, exhausted. My work ethic would become my saving grace, my forte.

The following week, I hung around after every practice session and ran an extra mile as my teammates raggedly walked away from the track. Built long and lean, I clicked my watch and tried to sprint the mile's four laps. Alone, unheeded, and with no desire to surrender to fatigue, my competitive instincts kicked in, and I found myself devouring the smooth stretch of rubber in front of me. My muscles moved and ached in a way that begged me to keep going, just to see how far I could push myself—always *one* step more. My speed improved rapidly, but perhaps more than fitness and stamina, I gained a certain reputation around school. Most of Regina, including the teachers, thought I was crazy.

Early on a gray, windy April afternoon, the track smelled like tar but felt like asphalt, as I warmed up for my first mile race. I asked my coach if I could use sprinters' blocks to start.

Mrs. Potts replied, "You're running the mile," then shook her head. "Pace yourself!"

Lining up with ten other ghost-faced adolescents, also stuck in the mile, I rocked from toe to toe, pondering over how I should pace myself. When the starter's pistol shot shattered the momentary silence, I charged ahead like I was running the 100-meter dash, determined to show my coach she was wrong. The harsh wind blasted my face, no matter in which direction I turned. Fortunately, a healthy dose of adrenaline had kicked in and I managed to weather the chill. After the first lap, I raced thirty yards ahead of the field. When the official flipped the lap counter to three laps remaining, a man in the crowded bleachers skeptically wondered aloud, "Does this kid know how long the race is?"

Sitting one row behind him, my mother silently asked herself the same question.

Bolting down the backstretch on the final circuit, I targeted a struggling, soon-to-be-lapped runner and mercilessly blew by him. Rounding the corner, I pushed hard through the finish line. Three steps later, I stopped, bent over and clasped my knees, panting uncontrollably. An official told me I had run 5:15. Later, I asked my coach if that was good. She said I had broken the school record by twenty-two seconds.

2. Legends of the Fall: September 1997

Two years later, a freshman in high school, I had grown accustomed to driving myself to exhaustion. Running far hurt! You had to understand that truth, absorb it, and get over it. During the summer, I had trained for my first season on the cross country team where we would race five kilometers over golf courses and town parks. We were ranked number one in Iowa and competition for the seven varsity spots proved tough. I stuck my nose in the workouts and quickly emerged as the team's second runner.

A few weeks later, I received my Regina uniform, a simple garment that carried a heavy burden. It demanded that I embody the tradition Coach Brown had established and nurtured during his ten years. Its pillars included "doing things the right way, even when no one is looking" and "putting the team before the individual". He declared that our Champion-brand uniforms were appropriate, because if we gave "nothing but our best", the boys' team had the potential to "do something special". What defined "special" for my teammates and me? A state championship.

When the final school bell rang on uniform day, I rushed to the weight room where a storage closet constructed of temporary wooden walls housed our jerseys. The seniors stood at the front of the line, the juniors next, and the sophomores behind them. I brought up the rear, packed in the cattle call of freshmen waiting to pluck their uniforms from a dusty laundry bin that hadn't seen daylight since the previous season.

Every Regina runner received the same gear: a jersey top, shorts, and a pair of rumpled warm-ups. When it was my turn, I greedily snatched the ill-sized cast-offs from the upperclassmen. I couldn't have been happier. Though our conservative navy and gold colors weren't flashy, our opponents had no trouble recognizing them. On biting cold days, other teams covered themselves in extra mismatching layers, but Coach Brown had decreed that no tights could be worn under our shorts nor long-sleeved shirts under our jerseys. Hats were for people who worried about the weather and Regina runners competed without a single nod of deference to Mother Nature.

"You can't control the weather," he would say, "you can only control *you*."

To shore up the tradition, Brown introduced the "Legends of the Fall" shirts that would subsequently become famous. The front of the shirt branded its wearer a "Legend of the Fall"; the back listed Regina's championship history, as well as the roster of state runners. If someone competed at state more than once, the corresponding number was added next to his name. Everyone, including those whose names weren't recorded on the back, owned one. The shirts became a source of pride in our team, a mark of distinction that proved how success built upon success. And they soon gained a following among non-runners, with moms and dads, and brothers and sisters of team members wearing them. Coach Brown felt that every person who had ever worn a Regina jersey should be called a "Legend of the Fall", regardless of whether his name was on the shirt or not. Treating all of his athletes, whether fast or slow, as equals was a hallmark of Coach's training ethic.

The concept of a "legend" held a different connotation for me. Long before I stood at the starting line of the state cross country meet my freshman year, shed my warm-ups and stocking hat and crouched down for the start, I had already decided I would become a "Legend of the Fall" the only way I knew how: I would win.

3. Practice at six a.m.: September 1997

The more I ran, the more I found myself falling in love with the sport. Running presented a rigorous test of will, given the physical endurance and mental fortitude it demanded. But at the same time, it offered me a release at the end of a stressful day, the chance to pound out any form of frustration with my legs. And, occasionally, during an easy afternoon jog, to muse about life or nothing in particular, as I mindlessly put one foot in front of the other. It gave me goals to meet, and an identity. I was known as the kid who ran fast. When I tired, I couldn't ask my coach to take me out of the race for a rest. Instead, I was left to find out if I had any grit or guts. I lived for that feeling.

By studying magazines and reading the latest news on the Internet, I became a student of the sport. I looked for allies on my Regina team who were wired the same way. During freshman year, I quickly learned that Coach Brown didn't necessarily embrace my single-minded ambitions. He followed mileage charts as a guide-line, but used a coaching tool that would never be found in any training manual: hugs. He was always pulling someone close, as if personal space didn't exist, and employing the power of touch to let them know he cared. While the hugs didn't do much for me, my teammates responded as much to them as they did to him.

One weekday in October, our team began its six a.m. cross country practices as usual. Headlights broke through the waning darkness and a caravan of cars filled Regina's parking lot. Showing up at school two hours before the first bell felt strange to everyone, but daily morning practices were the price of admission, a building block of our longstanding tradition. We rose early because we knew Coach Brown would be at school, waiting for us.

The team made its way inside Regina to the neon-lit, tiled hall-way between the lunchroom and the custodian's closet. Sitting on the floor, leaning against the walls, we waited. Some of my team-mates stared blankly at the whitewashed brick opposite them. Oth-ers rested their heads on their knees and let their heavy eyelids droop. Above us, the ceiling clock ticked 6:00. The coach, who guided, but never ran with us, walked around the corner, nodded toward the door, and said, "Let's go."

All thirty-four boys and girls (Brown coached both cross country teams during the fall, but only the boys' track team in the spring) shuffled outside and took their first step right in front of the parking lot's STOP sign. We warmed up during the one mile to the "church and back". Even though I had turned around at the Presbyterian church hundreds of times, I had never gone out of my way to find out its name. It was always, as Coach put it, "to the church and back."

When we returned to Regina, the captains led the stretching routine on the cold and craggy sidewalk in front of the building. The man already dressed in his work clothes, slacks and a button-down shirt, waded through our hyper-extended bodies, checking in with everyone. Warm and loose, we jogged behind the school and down the gravel hill to the track. Only then did the pendulum between darkness and light finally swing in our favor.

Surrounded by his loyal assistants, Coach Brown walked the team to the starting line for the workout: twelve arduous 400-meter sprints separated by a brief one-minute rest between each. Before we could set out, however, Coach made us pause: a teammate was turning sixteen and Brown had just realized that he had forgotten to mention it earlier. To make up for the oversight, he volunteered to lead everyone in a rendition of "Happy Birthday", before we started sweating.

Singing before a workout? It certainly was a heady start to the day.

Coach Brown had been to Regina's school Masses and knew that most students didn't sing in the middle of the afternoon. What would possibly motivate my teammates to do it at six-thirty in the morning? Undeterred, Coach seized the role of choir direc-tor, swinging his hands in the air and aggressively hitting the first "Haaaaa..." Everyone, from the self-conscious freshman girls to the cynical seniors, followed his lead, happily mashing a range of oc-taves into one jarring mess. I hastily mouthed bits and pieces of the words, sang out of tune, and skipped the final verse altogether. Feeling my muscles tighten, I tried surreptitiously to yank my right foot back to my butt and stretch my quads.

By the time the serenade ended, the team was in hysterics. Someone quipped, "That's why we're the running team, not the choir!"

Coach Brown caught me rolling my eyes. I noticed that, but didn't think too much of it. With his slowly receding hairline, his thick salt-and-pepper mustache, and the deep contours branching out from his eyes, he looked like the grandfather he was.

"What'd you do with the money your mom gave you?" he asked, loud enough for everyone to hear.

"Money for what?" I asked.

"For the singing lessons!" he fired back, laughing at his signature joke as if it were the first time he had hit the punchline. He had, in fact, used it on many, even good singers. I hadn't known that at the time.

I stared blankly into the crowd of my teammates, where smiles framed in braces were beginning to pop up on faces. My instincts told me that had any of my friends come up with such a joke, now would have been the time for sarcastic repartee. But glancing at Coach Brown and the weathered lines across his face, I sat back, relaxed. His lips were cracked open and dimples furrowed deep grooves in his cheeks. His solemn delivery couldn't hide his lively grin. It looked like there was no place he'd rather be at six-thirty in the morning than with thirty-four high school boys and girls forty years his junior. My teammates' glossy grins matched Brown's. Unmoved, I was the only person anxious to get started on the workout.

4.   Don't cut corners: April 1999

When I envisioned the Regina running tradition, the image in my mind included setting a cross country state championship record like we had done my freshman year. It did *not* include a basketball court. Whenever Coach Brown assigned easy days of jogging during my sophomore track season, the captain clandestinely led our distance crew to a teammate's house. Rather than complete the requisite forty-five-minute recovery run, my teammates played pick-up basketball games in the driveway. Coach had no idea what we were up to. Before practice, weekend runs, and the homecoming dance, his only instruction was: "Do things the right way, even when no one is looking." He gave us the tools, then left us to put them to work.

On basketball days, our distance group left Brown tending to his sprinters, throwers, and jumpers at Regina's track. The nine of us headed down First Avenue like a pack of gazelles, our springy legs blessed with youthful energy and forgiving knees. We positioned ourselves in order of seniority or according to who was the fastest in the group; the two often coincided. I had no problem leading a race or a hard workout. It was the only way to get my teammates to follow me. Easy runs, though, were a different story.

When we arrived at our teammate's house, I was the only one who didn't stop moving. The first time it happened, I couldn't believe the captain had turned the workout on its head and was flatly disobeying Coach Brown's instructions. My teammates had figured that playing basketball for forty-five minutes was the equivalent of running for the same amount of time. I knew that was far from the truth. So I jogged endless thirty-meter circles around the hoop, avoiding eye contact and biding my time until the orange ball surfaced. When my teammates began tossing it around, I didn't argue. I ran to Hickory Hill Park to carry out the day's assignment.

Whenever I faced a tough decision about training, my mind would flash back to the seventh-grade time trial. I remembered my teammates' lithe bodies taunting me as they sped away down the backstretch. The years had passed, but the importance of the lesson

I had learned then, of hard work having no substitute, remained fresh in my mind. I wanted to set records; so I acted accordingly, and often alone. If I was doing things the way I knew was right, why did I feel out of place, I wondered. Gliding over the packed dirt in Hickory Hill, I didn't allow myself to answer the question. Focused on the trail ahead of me, I simply kept running.

5. Paradise for $2.50: October 1999

Our cross country team had the chance to make history my junior year, an impressive prospect, considering that Coach Brown had won his first boys' team state championship in 1993. It had been a productive six years. Under his guidance during the past two, we had become the first small-school team to win back-to-back state championships in 1997 and 1998. As a result, Regina and Bob Brown had become household names across Iowa. As the team battled pre-race nerves in a pop-up tent, our temporary locker room, and waited for our section, Coach Brown took a few minutes for himself and indulged in the closest thing he had to a superstition: a limp, boiled hot dog, sold for $2.50 out of the back of the golf cart shed. In the middle of the fairway, before the biggest race of his career, Coach Brown devoured pure joy as the wind swirled around him. It seemed that if he ate a hot dog, his team would perform well. Regina had never finished below fourth place at the state meet. In our division of more than 150 teams, we had an unrivaled tradition.

The Lakeside Municipal Golf Course in Fort Dodge hosted the meet a few miles outside of town. A row of porta-potties marked "Athletes Only" separated the parking lot from the course. The lines for them ran four deep all day. Fifty feet in front of the bathrooms was the starting line. Chalky marks of white spray paint divided it into twenty-four boxes. It resembled the starting gate at a horse track; only, each tiny box was filled with all seven teammates, packed four deep like the toilet lines.

Minutes before our race, quite a few of the other twenty-three teams stood in front of their boxes and jumped up and down, pumping each other up by rhythmically chanting, "We are the Pi-o-neers! The might-eee, might-eee Pi-o-neers!"

Our team stood in a tight circle and locked arms around one another's shoulders. We looked to our coach who read our thoughts.

"It's okay to be nervous," he reassured us. "Everyone is going to have butterflies in their stomach before the state meet. You just have to make sure all of yours are flying in the same direction. Forward."

That brought grins to our faces. Right before 168 amped-up boys sprinted from the line en masse and funneled, sharp elbows flying, into a fifteen-foot-wide race path, Coach Brown quietly said, "Look at your teammates and repeat, 'If it's to be, it's up to me.'"

We did.

Then he asked, "What are you going to do to help the team?"

Each boy repeated the familiar words, "Give nothing but my best."

BANG!

As soon as it started, the 5k finished, so fast, in fact, that half of the field couldn't remember what had just happened. The spectators rushed over to the neon-orange plastic fence that separated them from the racers and began searching for their school colors. We were lost in a post-race world of our own, and it would take a few moments for us to return to life after seventeen minutes of fans constantly yelling, "You gotta want it! Catch that guy! You gotta go NOW!"—none of which we heard, because we had been focused solely on overcoming the pain that crippled our bodies and overtaking the guy in front of us. A few of my teammates inhaled deeply and tried to suck oxygen back into their heaving bodies.

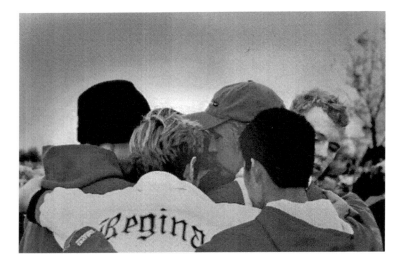

The team huddles around Coach Brown minutes
before the start of the state cross country meet.

Others, too tired to move, lay sprawled on the grass, limbs pointed in every direction like a downhill skiing wipe-out. I found myself pacing aimlessly, feeling my pulse throb in my arms, my fingers. Red-faced exhaustion was expected at the state meet. Tomorrow was a long year away or never, for seniors like Tony, our new captain. He had competed with a sense of urgency, finishing in the top ten. He had done his part to help the team win.

We knew the results were in when we heard the cheers—coming from another team: the new state champions. We were third, ten points behind the gold medalists. The results brought us back to cold, hard reality. We had lost. No one knew what to say. So we looked for Coach Brown. Sandwiched between fans, he was slowly making his way toward us. We couldn't see him, but he could see us, because he had noticed Tony standing to the side of our group, and David standing a few feet to Tony's left.

A quarter-miler by trade, David gutted out the taxing distance for the good of the team during cross country season. He was our fifth man, the final person to add to the team score. Before the race, Brown had called him the "DM" or "difference-maker". But while David should have catapulted past the competitors in the finishing straight, they had passed him. David felt he had let us down. His hands clasped on his head, he was staring into the puffy clouds, as if they held an answer to what had happened. Powerless, Coach could only watch from a distance as Tony sought out David.

When our captain drew near, David averted his eyes. Undeterred, the former wrapped his arm around his teammate's shoulders. Coach Brown could barely hear Tony as he said reassuringly, "Don't worry, David. You didn't let anyone down. I know you're upset with your race, but you gave your best. That's all the team asked for, and that's all you could do."

Only then did David let his hands fall from where they had been connected over his head. He made eye contact with Tony who reached out and folded his arms around David. Instantly, Coach Brown knew he had witnessed a moment more important than what could have been a third straight state championship. His captain had put people ahead of place—that took precedence over another team trophy any day. Looking at the scene from another angle, I had also observed all that had passed between Tony and David. The only difference was that I didn't know how I would have ranked people and place myself.

Tony, the captain, and Coach Brown
celebrate after the state meet.

6. Life on the range: October 1999

An hour later, Coach Brown gathered the entire boys' and girls' teams, including those who hadn't competed at the state meet. Together, he led us to join in one of the most unique Regina traditions: the "team hug". Coach used the yearly ritual to make us understand that after the races had been run, all that we would be left with was each other. Though he liked—loved—to win, he knew that champions graduated and gold trophies gathered dust with time. Shiny medals eventually lost their luster, and memories, however great, were intangible. None of these had the lasting power of a hug.

Off the back of the golf course's clubhouse lay a small pond, reflecting a murky gray from the gathering clouds. A pair of weaving parallel white lines curved around the water. Filled with surging runners and flanked by spectators just a while back, they were now deserted. While the rest of our competitors headed to the parking lot in the opposite direction, our entire team walked to the wide swath of fairway next to the pond. No instructions were issued. Coach Brown simply stood in the middle of our group and held out a hand. An upperclassman grasped it and held out his other hand for a teammate. Soon, everyone was clasping hands with the person on either side of them. Then, with Coach still staking out the center, we ran in ever-widening loops until the line curled around him like a cinnamon roll and spread outward in layers. The swarm squeezed toward Coach Brown who led the cheer, "Regals! Regals! Regals!"

The hug worked. Infectious smiles spread rapidly across the team. The racers had put in their best effort and that was all Coach asked of them. No one had a reason *not* to feel upbeat. Except me. A hug, however heartwarming, couldn't reverse our third-place finish. What was so good about giving "nothing but my best", if we didn't end the day victorious?

During the off-season that winter, I began searching beyond Iowa for other like-minded souls. In my attempt to challenge the best runners in the country, I strayed from Coach Brown's off-season training plan and created my own. The philosophy underlying it was simple: when in doubt, add more mileage, intervals, and strength sessions. Unfortunately, my regimen didn't bring me any closer to gold. Instead, it caused classic overuse injuries like Achilles tendonitis and IT Band Syndrome. Whenever one crept up on me, I bull-headedly chose running and limping over rest and recovery. Coach could only watch helplessly as I spent far too much of my high school career hobbled by leg pain. Yet, I would not heed his advice to have patience. Patience and balance were for people who had time to wait, I thought. I wanted to win immediately. Coach Brown and I tangled like a grizzled old cowboy with an unbroken colt. This had been, and would continue to be a common theme throughout high school: he trying to rein me in and me chomping at the bit, always looking too far ahead.

The runners I emulated were the Torres twins from Chicago. Jorge, older by ten minutes, had won the high school cross country national championship his senior year. His brother Edwardo had finished sixth. Then there was Dathan Ritzenhein from Rockford, Michigan, who would graduate as a two-time high school cross country national champion. He was my age and already ran eighty miles a week! All three had college scholarship offers to go wherever they wanted to. Jorge and Ed, two years older than me, had already made their decision. Dathan would choose the same place as the twins. It was no coincidence they all wanted to run for one coach: Mark Wetmore.

7. Wetmore showed up! August 2000

On the threshold of my senior year, I had narrowed my college search down to two equally granola institutions: Middlebury College in Vermont and the University of Colorado in Boulder. Gut instinct told me that I would reject the academically superior Middlebury. I was keen on testing myself against the best runners in the country and Division III Middlebury wouldn't offer me that opportunity. If I headed east, I would always look over my shoulder and wonder if I could have made it out west. While I had no idea why Coach Wetmore accepted walk-ons when he got guys like Jorge and Ed and Dathan, the superstars' presence didn't scare me away. It confirmed what I already knew: Wetmore was the right coach for me. The story I had heard about him shoveling the track after a snowstorm as a college student left little doubt that we shared the same passion. Had I been in his place, I would have acted the same way.

When Wetmore was a Rutgers University student in the late 1970s, a blizzard had blown into New Jersey one winter night. The temperature had hovered in the low twenties and the streets of Camden were empty. Roads, houses, and highways, along with the university's track, had lain buried under the piles of white powder. The very next morning, Wetmore, the twenty-three-year-old with a crew cut, had boarded the train and commuted to track practice. He carried a plastic shovel in addition to his spikes. A letter-winning middle-distance runner, Wetmore had known the oval would be under snow and had shown up an hour early to clear the first two lanes by himself. Practice was slated to start at ten. And at ten, he had warmed up alone, because none of his teammates or coaches had arrived. The thought of skipping practice just this once had never even occurred to him. He was completing his warm-up strides when the head coach's Cadillac, with the assistant coach riding shotgun, had slowly lurched through the slushy ice and pulled into the parking lot late. From the track, Wetmore had looked through the car's window and read the assistant's lips: "Oh shit! Wetmore showed up."

The big car had parked alongside the track. With the coach calling out the workout from the warmth of the driver's seat, Wetmore had begun his set of 200-meter repeats. After each interval, the electric window would slide down. "Twenty-eight five!" the coach would shout at Wetmore. Then the window would slide back up. Once, when Wetmore had jogged down the backstretch, he looked across at the Cadillac and saw his head coach finish a pull from a bottle. As Wetmore started his next sprint, the head coach had passed the bottle to his assistant.

8. The minimum standards: September 2000

I started my senior year championship quest as a new person. My freshman body that had broken down with injury had now grown into itself. Following Coach Brown's suggestion, I had adopted a lifting program called the "Russian Circuit". It helped to strengthen my scrawny chest, arms, and shoulders. Initially, I would consider my new six-foot, 145-pound body too thick for a sport where gaunt is considered beautiful. But I quickly felt the power it generated, especially late in races, when my rivals would tire and I could muscle past them. My appearance changed as well. I let my facial hair grow, sporting a rare patch of stubble at my strait-laced Catholic school where the norm was to be clean-shaven. My mother had buzzed my curly brown hair for ten years. Now I wore it long and untamed.

On a Monday afternoon in early September, I began my long-term pursuit that, until then, had been a fantasy stuck in the back of my mind. Dialing hesitantly, I made my first call to Coach

Wetmore to ask him what it would take to walk on. I thought the phone would never stop ringing until it finally clicked to his answering machine. I stumbled through my message, though I had rehearsed it a dozen times. Then I hung up and waited. I didn't hear back from Wetmore that night. Or the following afternoon. Soon, the days had stretched into a week. Nothing. I called again and found myself confronted with the same voicemail recording, sounding direct, eloquent, and far too busy to talk to me. What had I expected? Every other blue-collar runner in the country had also devoured *Running with the Buffaloes* from cover to cover. The line to talk to Wetmore about walking on was surely out the door.

In early October, I wrote him a letter. Two days later, I fired off an email. It said: *My name is Matt McCue and I'm from Iowa City, Iowa. Simply put, I want to run with the Buffaloes. Please let me know what it will take to make your team. I will do it. Last track season, I broke ten minutes for the two-mile. That's not a fast time, but...*

Coach Brown had also written a letter on my behalf, stating: *He's a good kid. He is the toughest runner I've ever coached.*

One week. Two. Three. No response. With my unofficial college visit coming up, I emailed Coach Wetmore again, asking for a ten-minute meeting or whatever time he could spare for me. No word. I convinced myself that the legendary coach was testing me with his silence, asking, "How bad do you want it?" Or perhaps he didn't care about a small-town runner from Iowa?

A few weeks later, my parents and I flew out to Colorado. Located in the heart of Boulder, the University of Colorado is considered one of the most architecturally beautiful campuses in the country. The matching stone buildings, with their distinctive red terra-cotta roofs, looked like they had been hand-cut from the majestic Flatiron Mountains that towered high above the city. After a lengthy orientation, my parents and I found the running offices next to the football field, hidden in the annex of Balch, a bare-bones field house that was home to an aging three-lane indoor track. My parents waited outside as I went in. The four generic offices were crunched into tight quarters hidden in, what was essentially, a hallway. I reminded myself to compliment Coach Wetmore on his office, even if it matched the rest of the drab décor.

A gold nameplate marked his black wooden door. Behind it, Wetmore's office was dark, his blinds closed, his door shut. His secretary startled me and told me the team had flown to a meet. I should return in a few days. What! I thought to myself, Coach Wetmore's gone? He's gone! That does me no good. I've chased him for two months, written letters, sent emails, made calls—traveled 800 miles! I can't speak with him later. I'll be back in Iowa!

But what could I do?

Thanking the woman, I forced a smile, hoping that she might put in a good word to him about "the nice boy from Iowa". In fact, I had prepared myself for such a catastrophe. I slid my pre-written note under the crack of Wetmore's door. It reminded him, yet again, that I would do whatever it took to compete for him. I left the room and found my parents outside.

"How'd it go?" asked my mother as we walked away from Balch. "Did he remember you from those letters you sent?"

"Not exactly…"

I proceeded to blame my parents for scheduling our visit during a weekend when Coach Wetmore was out of town. My mom retorted that when she booked our flights *four months ago*, she was thinking about cheap tickets, not his availability.

"But—" I stammered.

"But what, Matt? This is your thing, and, as I see it, you have two options: you can keep going. Or you can feel sorry for yourself because you didn't see Coach Wetmore and give up."

My mother had to be tough. My dream was on the line. I knew she was right, but I couldn't admit it. I would never feel sorry for myself. Or quit. Biting my lip, I gazed off into the distance. My parents and I continued in silence, in the direction of the Flatiron Mountains, now obscured by blizzard clouds.

Three weeks later, Colorado's assistant coach, Coach Drake, sent me a packet addressed to Matt *McQue*. I tore into it, ignoring the misspelling, and scanned the typed form letter once. Then I re-read the last paragraph. It said:

Enclosed you will find a list of performance standards for admittance to the program. Athletes that have not met the minimum standards should carefully reconsider their candidacy to CU. Our program cannot accommodate people who have not met these marks.

I snuck a peak at the walk-on standard for two-miles: 9:20. My best time was 9:55. I read the letter again, focusing on one sentence: *We hope you will choose to pursue joining our team.* The challenge slowly sank in. My walk-on attempt would be nearly impossible *and* someone from CU was aware of my existence. I immediately filled out the enclosed questionnaire.

9. It's kind of neat: October 2000

The bell signaled the end of Regina's school day as my team-mates and I spilled from the locker room and eased across the parking lot toward the yellow bus. Dressed for competition, our backpacks hugged our lean torsos and gym bags hung from our bony shoulders. The cross country postseason had arrived and the state-qualifying meet was being held in the rural town of Tipton, forty-five minutes away (in the Midwest, we judge distance in terms of driving time.) Only the top seven varsity boys would race, but because Coach Brown believed the entire team should travel together, the junior varsity runners also got on board. Freshmen filled the tattered front seats, while the seniors slumped in the prized back of the bus. I walked past my younger, slower teammates. Many wore their "Legends of the Fall" T-shirts. As everyone took their seats, the familiar pre-race smells—of bananas, a recent slap of deodorant, and the nose-clearing mintiness of menthol—pervaded the air.

Coach Brown was the last to join us. He wore his familiar navy and gold striped Regina polo tucked into blue jeans, a perfect fit for the unseasonably warm October day and the roll-up-your-sleeves nature of our sport. Standing between the front seats and facing us at the back, he flipped through his gym bag. Everyone knew what he was doing. He had done it many times, both this season and in years past. While the name would be different, the theme would be the same: a former Regina runner would have used the lessons they learned from Coach to help them overcome one of life's many trials.

"I got something today," said Coach Brown, holding up a letter. "Many of you probably don't know the person who wrote it, but he ran for Regina a long time ago. I want to read part of it to you." He began, quoting from the letter. *I'll tell you, this job stuff is hard. I thought it was hard on those days when we had to go to school after a set of Hickory Hill 800s, but rounds at the hospital are a new kind of hard. What really gets me through the day is what you taught me; things like, 'Nothing but my best' and 'If you think you can or you think you can't, you're right'. Thank you.*

Coach looked back at us. "I wanted to share that with you," he explained, "because he's going to become a doctor and he still uses the quotes we always talk about. I think it's kind of neat and, remember, you all are a part of it." "Neat" was one of Brown's trademark adjectives. In one swift motion, he stuffed the letter back in his bag, sat behind the wheel, fired up the engine, and pulled the hand lever to shut the door. He looked both ways and stepped on the gas.

• • •

Coach Brown was literally the driving force behind our team.

Districts didn't end as I had hoped. In an attempt to set the meet record, I had blasted from the starting line like an amateur trying to win the 3.1-mile race in the first half mile. I went from running tall, upright, and in the lead to dancing the skeleton dance on my way to a dismal seventh place out of 126 runners. Although the team had qualified for state, we finished in second place, twenty-nine points behind Tipton. Unhappy, both with my performance and that of our team, I fell into a snit.

Afterwards, Coach Brown told the boys' team to cool down two miles to shake the soreness from our legs while he picked up the results packet. The varsity seven jogged to the far edge of Tipton's town park, which had served as the course. A ball field was to our left, a drainage ditch and one-lane road to our right. Across the road was a harvested cornfield; a barbwire fence marked its boundary. With most of the trees starkly rising from the carpet of wrinkled red, orange and yellow leaves they had shed, there was little refuge to be had from the late afternoon sun.

After receiving our manila envelope of clinking silver medals at the award ceremony, I led my six teammates. Minutes into our cool-down, my emotions still pulsing, I impulsively whipped around to face them, thrust the burdensome envelope in their faces, and brought everyone to a sudden halt. My hands thrashed as wildly as the words that spilled from my lips, triggered by the thoughts that swept through my competitively fired-up mind. Speaking from the heart, I began, "Guys, these silver medals are a challenge! One that asks—no, begs—us not to settle for them! They taunt us by what they stand for! They mark us as…losers! I see them as additional motivation! We need to think for ourselves, dare to have our own opinions, and not let our minds be influenced by what society deems successful! If we have more fight in us—if we want it more—these medals can motivate us to win state! Something must be done! Second place is not success!"

I scanned our surroundings and spontaneously started toward the cornfield. I poured the medals into my hands, took two swift steps, wound up, and chucked them high into the air. They flew across the road, cleared the barbwire fence, and landed with a clunk on the field's calloused dirt. I had thrown away the source of our disappointment, our embarrassment. Vindication!

I turned back to my teammates, expecting to be met with expressions of awe and admiration. What greeted me was silence. Two of our teammates abandoned our cool-down and made a beeline to the cornfield. I ignored them and continued running ahead. Unsure of what to do, my other four teammates hesitantly fell in line behind me. I felt the two who had left us were content with what I regarded as a defeat. I would not stop to indulge that attitude. As they scavenged for their silver treasures among the fallen stalks, I led the rest of the guys back to the empty Regina bus, the only one left in the lot.

We arrived to find the rest of our team sprawled on the cool, shaded grass next to the bus, using gym bags as pillows, waiting to go home. The post-race snacks of Jell-O eggs and bagels had been consumed and fatigue had set in. As I picked through the remnants of the treats, I heard the whispers circulating about our two remaining teammates who weren't back yet. Those who hadn't actually seen me throw the medals couldn't accept the truth at first. I heard exclamations of incredulity above the chatter: "Matt did what? No way!"

Three people soon emerged from between a pair of thick oaks in the distance. And a single glance told everyone that the rumors were indeed true. My two teammates carried their dusty medals tightly gripped in their fists. Their eyes were swollen, their red faces burned. Coach Brown trailed one step behind, a hand on each boy's shoulder. A sacred silence had descended on the team, much like the kind that fills the split second between a race starter's announcement, "On your marks," and the firing of the gun. While the two boys walked with their heads bowed, Coach stared unblinkingly at one person. Me. I knew it was a matter of mere seconds before the command came—

"*Matt* McCue! I need to speak with you!"

I shot up as Coach Brown looked to either side, trying to find a suitable spot where he could conduct his conversation with me, undisturbed. We were in the middle of the empty parking lot. The bus offered the only cover. "Come with me," he said, firmly gripping my bicep, displaying the strength he normally reserved for hugs. When we were alone on the other side of the vehicle, he let me hear it.

"Who are you to define their success? To say their best isn't good enough!"

Looking him in the eye, I grunted, "I'm sorry," every time he paused for breath during his five-minute tongue-lashing.

He finished, "Fast or slow, first, second or last, I DON'T CARE! You're a Regina runner. We do things the right way, NO MATTER WHAT! "

I nodded, but my thoughts were elsewhere. All I could think about was winning the state championship ten days later. Coach Brown finished with, "We both know you're better than this."

"I know," I said, apologizing to him and to my teammates. But inside, nothing had changed. That night, I drove home on the country roads veiled by the darkness in which I often ran. The eight-mile ride gave me plenty of time for reflection. I realized that despite all that had happened, I felt not one ounce of remorse.

Coach Brown instills advice in me the only
way he knows how to, up close and personal.

10. Buffaloes on the plains: November 2000

A month after I had thrown out the medals, the 2000 NCAA Cross Country National Championships were held in Ames, Iowa, on the rim of Iowa State University's campus. The pundits considered the course, with its green open space, rolling hills, and wooded patches, one of best in the nation. Iowa's November weather was the wildcard factor. Bone-chilling gusts stormed through the state on Monday morning and the single-digit wind chill threatened to spoil the day for the hundreds of collegiate hopefuls who had traveled from places like Arizona, Arkansas, and California.

My parents had granted me, along with my brothers and my sister, a reprieve from school. So our entire family drove to Ames. Coach Wetmore and his Buffaloes would be there. I would finally have the chance to introduce myself. One hour before the men's championship race, I stepped from our Chevy van and started toward the thick of the action. A roaring blast of razor-sharp air immediately tore into my exposed cheeks. I combed the frozen expanse, watched the athletes stride past, and searched for the trademark black and gold of Colorado. Nearly six hundred fans had shown up; most were packed near the starting line. I preferred to watch from the depths of the course.

The remote section half a mile away from the crowds was where I would spy Coach Wetmore, traversing the far border alone wearing a jet-black Colorado jacket. Waiting for the race to begin, I stood next to a handful of fans huddled together for warmth. Wetmore walked by us without slowing down, and stopped just ten feet away. I glanced his way and noticed the lines that had weathered his face. It was as if each one told a story about withstanding the rigors of a day such as this. The lone wolf stood tall, his arms crossed tight over his chest, his eyes deep-set, his scowl deeper still. The wind whipped his thin ponytail this way and that. On his feet were the most rugged, scuffed pair of leather workman's boots I had ever seen.

The race starter's pistol cracked in the distance. Three minutes later, hundreds of fit men passed directly in front of us. A number of brave ones wore shorts; others preferred tights and long sleeves; all had chafed rosy cheeks and watery eyes. I watched Coach Wetmore as he observed the majority of his Colorado team pulling up the rear. Under the clompclompclomp of the spikes smacking the hard ground, his voice was calm: "You're fine, men. You're fine. Heads up. Be patient." His tone was eerily reminiscent of the way Coach Brown spoke amid the silence of the grass and the hills.

Heeding such advice and exercising the desired patience proved to be wise for Wetmore's men's team. It propelled them to second place behind the University of Arkansas. Individually, Jorge Torres had finished third. Earlier in the day, in a separate race, Coach Wetmore's women had won the team championship and his phenom, Kara Grgas-Wheeler, had claimed the individual crown.

After the race, I found the Colorado team near the T-shirt stand. Their celebration was in full swing despite the weather taking another turn for the worse. The sky spat light flakes that were kicked around by the howling wind. The Buffaloes were too busy hugging and high-fiving to notice. Their challengers had already loaded up their team vans and left, fantasizing, no doubt, about a steaming hot shower at the hotel before flying far from Iowa.

I stood at the fringe of Colorado's lively mob like a groupie, waiting to pounce the minute Coach Wetmore surfaced. I was finding it difficult to catch him at the right moment. He always seemed to be in conversation with one of the thirty people firmly rooted inside the ring of bundled bodies. The thought of leaving had briefly crossed my mind. But I knew that if I did, I would, in all likelihood, sacrifice my walk-on chances. I needed to show him the face that went with my name, so I stayed on, dismissed the weather, and waited for my turn. Finally spotting him alone, I discreetly walked around the perimeter of the charmed circle and stopped two feet from him, facing the man who was already a legend in my mind.

"Coach Wetmore, hi," I began, "I'm Matt McCue, and good job, your teams ran well today and...uh, I've written you about walking-on, and I want to be a Buffalo...and...uh... Well, I just thought that since I live in Iowa and saw you here, I would introduce myself....Jorge ran really well today, huh..." I offered my hand and pretended not to notice that my wool mitten was smeared with the snot I'd been wiping from my face all morning. It didn't help that my grip was much stronger than his frozen one and that I forcefully drove back his hand as if we were arm-wrestling.

Wetmore accepted my outstretched, covered hand, but said nothing.

I rushed in to fill the silence. "Sorry about the weather," I continued, "Usually, it's not this bad. Today was just a freak day. Yesterday, the sun was out! Perfect for a hard ten miles!" I didn't mention I had only run six.

He looked past me. I stood directly in front of him, matching his serious demeanor, unsure as to whether I should reintroduce myself or if I had caught him at a bad time—or why in the world wasn't he responding?

The reply finally came.

"Okay. Thanks for introducing yourself, Matt McCue."

Okay? Just okay?

A Colorado runner's mother came up to congratulate Coach Wetmore. Though I badly wanted to protect my turf and keep her off it, I passively watched him turn to converse with the woman. As he accepted her congratulations for his current victory, I noticed he had that faraway look, as if he were already thinking about next year's national championship run. The expression was familiar. Leaving the Colorado group, I rejoined my family in our van.

"How'd it go?" my mother asked. "What'd he say? Did he remember you from your letters?"

"Well..." was all I could come up with.

11. Running wild — Brown's way: February 2001

The February sky was hidden under a perpetual cloud of gray; winter's dreariness had lingered far too long. The school day had ended. Regina's halls were quiet, except for the twenty-five boys, myself included, who had stuck around for the pre-season track meeting. We sat at the plastic brown lunch tables in the cafeteria while Coach Brown outlined his plans for the upcoming months. He explained that with spring break and the senior trip to Washington D.C., each of us needed to make the right decisions away from the team. As the only class member who hadn't signed up for the senior trip, I knew I wasn't going anywhere other than to track practice.

Brown sprinkled his speech with quotes from his usual arsenal. "Whether you think you can or you think you can't, you're right," or "The deed's in the doing, not in the saying." After hugs, quotes were his next most powerful coaching tool. He borrowed them from a wide range of sources that covered both Henry Ford and Volkswagen commercials. He walked around among us, speaking so softly and slowly that we had to lean toward him to hear what he was saying. Twenty minutes later, he clapped his hands and concluded, "I think we're going to have a fun year. Thanks for coming, guys."

Dressed in tights and a fleece, I turned and walked toward the door. Behind me, I heard Coach razzing a shot put thrower. "You're a senior. Practice starts in three days. Why in the world haven't you turned in your physical waiver yet?"

On a normal weekday, I changed into running gear, stretched and headed out the door by three-thirty. It was four o'clock now, but I was adamant that the late start or the snowstorm forecast for the evening would neither disrupt my run today nor my goals for the future. After the unsatisfactory way my cross country season had finished four months earlier, goals were all I had to keep me going. Despite my throwing away the silver medals and reaching for state championship gold, I had raced to third place. Coach Brown had motivated the team to overperform and we had finished second, handily defeating Tipton who had beaten us at Districts.

After the state race, Coach told me he was proud of my effort. I looked away. Eyes downcast, my windblown hair awry, I replied through gritted teeth, "I. Didn't. Win." With easy camaraderie, he put his arm around my shoulder and stared at the frozen ground alongside me. "I know," he said, his voice just above a whisper, "but you should feel good. How many guys beat you at Tipton?"

"Six," I replied.

"And how many of them did you come back and beat today?" He answered for me, "All of them. I know you're not happy, but I am, because you fought back and battled. You gave your best and that's what matters most."

Coach Brown catches me after the state meet, and
reminds me how I still succeeded even though I didn't win.

Now Coach Brown had my ear again. He caught me before I could make it out of the cafeteria and asked about my off-season training. I told him it had gone fine, just fine. I withheld the fact that it had been the best of my life.

"Matt," he said, resting a hand on my shoulder. "I've been thinking about you a lot lately. This is *your* senior year, *your* last season. I've decided it's time to let you run wild, but you have to run wild on *my* terms." He had poked my chest twice with his index finger when he rhythmically emphasized, "My terms."

Thoughts of a failed cross country campaign rushed my senses. I paused. "Okay," I agreed. Whatever that meant.

"All right. Once practice starts next week, no more hammering your Saturday morning long runs by yourself. From now on, it's you and me. We'll meet at nine."

I still had no idea what he meant. Was he going to train with me? Were we to run side by side up a hill? For three years, I had never completely followed Coach Brown's plan, always tinkering with it and adding more mileage and intensity wherever I saw fit. For the first time in my life, I trusted him.

"Okay," I concurred, then repeated his words after him. "From now on, it's you and me."

12. I'll be there: April 2001

At the end of April, I stood in my family's laundry room and stared at the black numbers typed upon the white sheet. Ever since I had received the performance standards from Coach Drake, running 9:20 for two miles had been my benchmark—the gateway to Colorado. It also reminded me of the Buffaloes' elite status. A 9:20 for two miles would have been fast enough to earn at least a partial scholarship to nearly every other college in the nation. At Colorado, it was only good enough for *consideration*. I had read about athletes who taped their goals to their bedroom walls for inspiration. I went one step further and buried that time deep in my mind. I wanted to see it during every run, every class period, and every night in my dreams. That worked. One spring evening in early April, I had popped a big race and lowered my two-mile best by twenty-five seconds down to 9:30. I was now on the cusp of consideration.

With a shot of credibility to bolster my position, I dialed Coach Drake to alert him to my improvement. Though he had sent the packet of walk-on guidelines, I could tell he didn't recognize me. He probably got ten calls like mine every day from athletes hoping to talk their way into Colorado. When I asked him about the steps following graduation, he elaborated in his emotionless drawl, "Our guys spend the summer training here in Boulder. If you are still serious about making the team, you should really move here by July to get acclimatized and train with them."

"Okay," I replied. "I'll be there."

I'll be there. The words had left my mouth even before I realized what I had said. I had no friends in Boulder, nowhere to stay. I didn't have a job waiting or a car to drive to Magnolia Road. And what did "summer training" even mean? I would be running with the best guys in the country, a prospect as terrifying as it was exhilarating. As far as I was concerned, my move was set in stone. I *would* be there.

That night, I called my Aunt Sarah who lived in Nederland, a mountain town thirty minutes west of Boulder. I begged her to allow me to live in her basement for the summer. She replied that I was welcome to, and that I would have a room to myself, but I'd have to share a bathroom with my three cousins, all girls under the age of eleven.

Soon after this conversation, I told my summer boss that I had to leave at the end of June. I was moving to Boulder.

"What are you doing going out there so early?" she asked.

"I'm chasing my dream."

13. Have yourself a day! May 2001

The overcast final day of the 2001 Iowa Boys' State Track Meet gave hundreds of fellow athletes the chance to put the finishing touch to their seasons or, like me, to high school careers. Held at Drake Stadium in Des Moines, the meet would be defined by one other color besides gold: blue. For the tradition-rich track tucked within the storied brick stadium was known for its unique sky-colored surface.

Early on Saturday afternoon, I left Drake's indoor warm-up area and made my way to our team camp in the wooden bleachers. Before heading for the line demarcated for the 1600-meters, I sat on the concrete aisle steps next to Coach Brown and listened to his pre-race instructions for the final time.

"You know what to do," he said, placing his arm around my shoulder.

"Yeah," I replied.

"Remember, this is the state meet. Everyone has a kick with 200 to go. Make your move with 400 left. It's your last race. Nothing but your best."

I nodded and rose to my feet.

"Have a day!" he said, swinging his right hand at my stomach like a tennis racket—whack! It was a slap square in the gut, an extension of what was known within the team as a "Coach Brown love tap". The problem was that Coach tended to underestimate his own strength. His show of affection literally took my breath away. More than once, he had unknowingly knocked the wind out of me, throwing me into a world of panic right before a race. By the time

I became a senior, I had learned my lesson. I now met with Coach long before the first call.

As in all distance races at the state meet, practically every boy in the twenty-four-person field charged out too aggressively at the gun. Pacing myself, I was left at the back of the pack, where I drafted and conserved my energy. The leaders hit sixty-six seconds for the first lap, a 4:24 mile pace. I came through in sixty-eight; two seconds was a huge gap. Confident that no one in the race matched my fitness level, I moved up over the second lap and put myself near the front, splitting 2:15 for 800 meters. Halfway done—it was always about being *done*. The pace remained honest over the third lap. I pushed into second place and stalked the leader.

When the frontrunner drifted into lane two, I knew he was tiring. So I surged to the lead with 500 meters to go. Now I was the hunted. As in a chess match, the next move was mine. It had to be decisive—race-defining. If not, there was a line of wolves right behind me, ready to overtake me at any moment. Five of us were still in contention with one lap—the bell lap—remaining. The clock said 3:28.

Before the bell clanged, I unleashed a devastating kick around the turn that shot me forty yards—a lifetime in the 1,600—ahead of the field. I powered down the backstretch and around the far turn, where bystanders wildly cheered...for my competitor from Newman Catholic Mason City, who had caught me and was locked on my shoulder. When he pulled even in the homestretch and gained a few inches on me, I wanted to grab his shoulders and physically hold him back. He couldn't win, I told myself. This was *my* race. The last thirty meters were a blur...

DIVE! I crashed to the track, face down, arms and legs scattered in an untidy heap. Dead.

It had been so close that I had thrown myself at the finish line.

I dragged my heaving body up from the blue surface and noticed how the rubber had eaten chunks of skin from my knee and elbow. My eyes, and those of my competitor, zeroed in on the scoreboard and waited for the longest minute of my life. The results were posted—a miniscule 0.08 seconds separated first and second place. Four years of hard work boiled down to the blink of an eye. Jesus, it was so close... I couldn't imagine losing. When "ICR" flashed next to #1, I lifted my arm in a salute to victory, lost in the rush of teammates who had left the stands to surround me. I had run 4:27.88 and won because I had lunged at the line and my competitor had not. In my own eyes, the results proved that I had redeemed myself completely and made up for all the near misses and second-place finishes. For once, I didn't yearn for tomorrow, for the next win. I was going out a champion.

I walked back to the bleachers and spotted Coach Brown. He greeted me with outstretched arms and gathered my spent body into them, refusing to let go. I hugged him back and the tension slowly eased from my shoulders. The loner in me didn't want to admit it, but his embrace was unexpectedly comforting.

After all of the miles I had posted in training, I was surprised that the race had come down to a sprint. Coach had known better, which was why on our Saturday mornings together, he had let me run wild, but on his terms. He had cut down my normal long run from thirteen miles to twelve. In order to strengthen my finishing kick, he had replaced my last mile on the road with sixteen 100-meter sprints on the track. After just ripping a fifty-nine-second last lap, now would have been the perfect moment to admit to him that he was wiser than I had thought. Arms wrapped around him, I said all I needed to with my firm embrace. Then I sat down in the row directly in front of him, with his hands resting on my shoulders. The happiest guys in the stadium, we had finally found common ground. I didn't know what Coach Brown was thinking, but I savored the moment, instead of analyzing my performances over the past four years or planning them for the next four. A feeling of such complete fulfillment didn't come around very often. I snatched it up and held it close, unwilling to relinquish even an ounce of it.

But when the sun rose the next morning, the euphoria had passed. Magnolia Road shone on the horizon and beckoned me west.

II. BOULDER

The Transition

I. Running my guts out: July 2001

I arrived in the dry heat of Colorado with a well-thought-out plan. One week earlier, I had followed Coach Drake's advice and called Jorge Torres. He told me that the team ran together three days a week during the summer, meeting at seven-thirty a.m. at Potts, the university's track, and that I was welcome to join them on the very first morning after my arrival.

I told Jorge I'd be there. After I hung up, I realized I had forgotten to ask him for directions. Instead of calling back and risking sounding like a rookie, I spent the next week checking maps and emailing Boulder running clubs, seeking out anyone who might know the track's location. Finding Potts proved more difficult than I had imagined. Apparently, it wasn't an Internet search away. The closest I came to an "exact" location was an area of two square miles and numerous side streets deep in the heart of Boulder. With such paltry info in hand, I gunned my aunt's jeep out of her Nederland driveway at six on a Friday morning and began the twenty-five-minute drive down Boulder Canyon. I didn't want to be late, especially not on my first day.

The rising sun cut through the sleepy haze and needled pines as I steered down the canyon's steep and windy turns and pulled into sun-drenched Boulder. The Flatirons rose in the west. The dry land seemed to stretch for miles, uninterrupted, but for the cookie-cutter housing developments that spread unceasingly from Denver. I figured I would find the track next to the campus. So I headed in that direction. I had one hour to search. The adventure had begun. Surprising though it may have seemed, I didn't nervously wonder if I would be able to keep up with the Buffaloes on my first day. That issue had been settled long ago in my mind. A few times in my life, I had simply decided that I was going to do something. And I had. Today, I planned to physically *will* myself to stay with the Colorado runners, no matter what. I had to show them I belonged.

As I drove through the quiet streets, I thought about my former Regina classmates. They were back in Iowa, hanging out together for one last summer before leaving for college in the fall, where they planned to attend schools within a half-day's drive of Iowa City. I felt a bit smug about taking such a huge leap on my own while they stayed back at home. Seen as somewhat of a loner during high school, the guy who eschewed the popular crowd and skipped the senior-year drinking parties, I had preferred the relatively more sedate option—excelling in sports and academics, hanging out with my girlfriend and leading junior high retreats. Some of my former Regina classmates had described my mid-summer move as "gutsy". They had admitted that they themselves would never have tried it. Perhaps, the reason had something to do with their practical nature, as they wisely, patiently stepped into their future. That had never been my style. I needed the challenge, and I believed I could handle the outcome of plunging into the biggest one of my life. The question remained: what would it hand me?

Seven-thirty-two. The gravel crunched as I sped into Potts' parking lot, silently cursing myself for arriving late. I had finally found Colorado's track, which, as a training staple of a distance running powerhouse, looked a little, well, bare. The weatherworn crimson surface could have been mistaken for any track in America. Nothing in particular marked it as the home of champions. Located half a mile from campus and adjacent to an office park, the track appeared to have been randomly dropped into the urban landscape, far away from Colorado's massive football stadium. Surrounded by a chain-link fence, the track shouldered two outbuildings—an equipment shed and a concrete hut that housed the track's bathrooms and the locker rooms of Colorado's ski team. I guessed the ruggedness appealed to Coach Wetmore. It showed that being great couldn't always be measured in terms of fancy equipment, but often boiled down to the simple fact of working harder and being smarter than the rest.

Coach Drake had made it clear that the summer runs, led by Jorge, were optional. They weren't official practices. I figured that at least half a dozen other walk-on hopefuls would also show up. They would have found directions and arrived early, lowering my chances even before I had stepped out of the car. Much to my surprise, I saw only three men in attendance, their faces instantly recognizable: Jorge. Edwardo. Dathan. Dear God.

Shirtless, they stretched on the track. I walked up to them, extended my hand, and said, "Hey, I'm Matt McCue…the guy from Iowa. I'm hoping to walk on this year."

As they introduced themselves, I thought, I know who you guys are. I have tapes of your famous races in my archives! I had studied their training habits and memorized their personal records. Now I was about to run with them. Not a bad first day! For the first time in four years, I didn't start my usual stretching regimen. Instead, I mirrored their every move. As I touched my toes, I glanced in their direction, curious as to what made them so fast. They wore the newest Nike Air Maxes. I had Asics. Their washboard abs looked chiseled from stone. Their calves were impossibly slender, the veins nearly bursting out of the skin. I felt like a giant standing next to these real-life stick figures.

"Ready?" Jorge asked, as we finished stretching.

"Yeah," I replied, tossing my shirt on the ground next to theirs. "How far do you have to go?" asked Jorge.

Six miles, I thought to myself; that was easy. I had my weekly volume precisely calculated.

"We're going twelve," Jorge said, before I could answer.

"Good, me too," I replied.

Jorge led the four of us west along the Boulder Creek path, a cement trail that paralleled Boulder Creek and divided the town. When he accelerated the pace in the foothills, my lungs greedily sucked in the thin air. My legs felt as heavy as the boulders I barely managed to leap over. My arms boxed the breeze like those of a floundering lightweight on the ropes. Jorge, Ed, and Dathan, on the other hand, looked like they were coasting on autopilot. Screw the pain, I thought, I'm running with the Buffaloes! But these weren't just *any* Buffaloes. They were the best. I needed to hang tough and prove myself.

We descended from the foothills and connected to a new concrete path. Disoriented, I had an additional incentive to keep up with the skinny Trinity. I didn't want to get lost. Minutes later, we emerged from an underpass. Thankfully, I saw Potts Track a quarter mile away. I devoted all my efforts to extracting one last surge of energy from my nearly depleted reserves.

We flew past Potts as if it didn't exist. Apparently, stopping had never been an option.

Jorge glanced back at me and said, "We have to add another ten minutes to get our twelve miles, but you can go back if you want."

Every cell in my body wanted to scream, "I will!" I had already run more than ten miles when I should have stopped at six! By now, the drastic rise in elevation from the Iowa flatlands had caught up with me. It felt like someone were slowly tightening a noose around my neck. But I knew I would keep going. Gamely, I latched onto their pack, desperately trying to shift the focus away from my innards which felt like they were exploding from my midsection.

We returned to Potts ten minutes later, having run twelve miles in seventy-five minutes, a merciless pace, given the steep mountains and the mile-high altitude. Unlike the other three who looked fresh and unruffled, I walked through the chain-link fence with salt-crusted shorts, a flushed face, and the taste of cotton lingering in my mouth.

"*You* must be Matt McCue."

I recognized the forthright tone before I saw the trademark ponytail, the weathered demeanor, and the white socks hiked high past the ankles. His Nike Dri-Fit shirt tucked tightly into his gray nylon running shorts left me in no doubt. Coach Wetmore. He spoke like a man who had discovered his voice years ago. I always introduced myself with a strong, firm handshake, but the coach, leaning on a stretch of wooden railroad ties next to the track, kept his fingers intertwined on his lap.

"You made it," he continued. "Not everyone does. Now, don't try and hang with those three every day or you'll kill yourself."

"Okay," I replied, incredulous that Wetmore had somehow remembered my name. If he had said instead, "Kill yourself by trying to hang with those three every day," I would have agreed to do so instantly. In fact, I would have agreed to whatever he suggested. He then turned to Dathan and the Torres brothers, asking them how their summer training was coming along. I stood outside their huddle, imagining how I would describe the morning to my family. I could see their jaws drop at the mere mention of Coach Wetmore,

Dathan and the Torres twins. I planned to skip the part about getting lost and arriving late.

For the rest of the summer, only one other walk-on hopeful, Colorado native Travis Macy, attended every workout. Like most distance runners, he marched to a different rhythm—his own. Tall and muscular, with long blond hair, Travis was built more like me than like Dathan and the Torreses. He spoke in sentences liberally punctuated with exclamation points, confirming that he was "stoked!" about everything, from running *up* a mountain to his rusty red Toyota truck. He distinguished himself by, among other quirks, his lemon-colored athletic socks printed with little red critters crawling all over them. I took one look at Travis's feet and figured I had him beat. But while the little red bugs did nothing to help him fit in, his toughness did.

The first time Travis ran with us, he destroyed me and hung with Jorge, Ed, and Dathan, when they were humming, leaving me worried. Still, he remained my second most challenging walk-on opponent. I was my greatest foe. Despite the constant bludgeoning from the likes of the Colorado crew, I committed to a hard ten miles—fourteen on Sunday—whenever I ran with the team. The other days of the week, I ran on my own. The Colorado runners didn't take days off; so I followed their lead and gave up my one rest day a week. My "off" day now consisted of five miles. I consciously walked a fine line between breaking through to the team and breaking down with an injury that might well crush my dreams. The trade-off was worth it. Since Coach Wetmore controlled my destiny, I hoped to show him that I was willing to do whatever it took to become a Buffalo. Running my guts out seemed like the obvious first step.

2. If you give your best: August 2001

After one particularly draining fourteen-mile death march, I lounged on my aunt's deck, my body feeling heavy in the wooden chair as the high noon sun roasted me. My digestive system was in tatters, the result of efforts to replenish my nearly 2,000 burned calories by eating a breakfast fit for three, and continuously shoving fried eggs and toast, cereal and spoonfuls of peanut butter into my mouth. For the first time since I had left Iowa, I allowed myself to reminisce about my past glories at Regina. It didn't take me long to realize that one other person seemed to be present in every memory: Coach Brown.

He and I had taken our last trip together in mid-June, one month before I flew west. We had traveled to the Senior Spotlight, a post-season track meet for graduates from Iowa, Illinois, Wisconsin, and Nebraska held in Dubuque, Iowa. Coach Brown had been asked to guide the Iowa team; I had been invited to run. Having started the season way back in March with our Saturday morning workouts, it seemed fitting for us to finish together. The gently rolling hills and green forests had flown by outside as Coach drove me the two hours to Dubuque, a riverside community known for its Catholicism and gambling boats. Our forty-year age gap might have made for an odd pairing and strained conversation. But it didn't bother me. I had grown accustomed to him expressing equal interest in my mileage and my life. My former coaches had merely scratched the surface of the latter, only asking about my life outside of the sport in relation to how it impacted my performance. Brown, on the other hand, blurred the definition of "coach" by taking an interest in the person first and the runner second. For instance, he had asked about my parents on this trip. Before I could answer, he had remarked that while a lot of people "talked the talk", my mother was among the few who "walked the walk" by baking cookies for the team and making yard signs for the runners going to state. He had mentioned how appreciative he was that my dad hauled the team tent to every meet. Listening to Coach Brown, I had thought it sounded like his running programs were built much more like a family than a team.

Finally, after speaking about my parents, I had turned the focus to me. Coach and I hadn't discussed my walk-on goals during the regular season, because he put the team's needs before mine. I had then asked him what he thought about my chances. As we pulled into Dubuque, he had looked me in the eye and said confidently, "If you give your best, I believe you can make the Colorado team."

Daydreaming on my aunt's deck, I let the memory sink in. Coach Brown was the only person who had told me outright that he believed I could make it. But instead of telling him how much that meant to me, I had looked at the road ahead and replied, "Me too."

3. The story of the butterfly: September 2001

After two months of acclimatizing myself to the altitude, race day arrived. Colorado's five-mile time trial race over Labor Day weekend was the chance for Coach Wetmore to choose his walk-ons. The move west, the daily ten miles, and the sweaty effort boiled down to being a proving ground that the coach used to determine which potential walk-ons had the "stomach for the fight".

The Buffalo Range, Colorado's cross country course, was located in South Boulder, about three miles from campus on an arid stretch of dirt covered with rocks and prairie grass. When the latter was overgrown, Wetmore would cut it with a push mower. (I'd guess that no other NCAA Division I national championship coach had to mow his own athletic field.) The Buffalo Range's figure-eight loop featured an array of difficult surfaces: precipitous hills, grating slopes, rough edges, and loose-gravel flats that seemed endless.

Warming up, I tried to act as if the race looming ahead was like any other. Hah! The butterflies in my stomach were flying backwards, upside down, doing tailspins—moving in every direction, *but* forward. Originally, I had thought the racecourse made two-mile loops around the mud flat on the far lip of the 300-acre open space. That had changed three days earlier, when Travis and I walked into Coach Wetmore's office to ask for a course map. He had given us a computer printout that looked like a child's finger painting. Lines of every color collided with each other in one indecipherable mess. According to Wetmore, the interconnected segments marked the course. Both Travis and I were enrolled in Honors classes; yet when we arrived at the Buffalo Range, we promptly got lost trying to follow the map. What I had believed to be the course was actually a random trail not affiliated with the Buffalo Range at all.

Fifteen minutes before race time, I mentally noted the unknown collegians that made their way to the starting line. The growing number of walk-on hopefuls, about fifteen, was my competition. They hadn't run with the team during the summer, but I still worried about the guy who might come out of the woodwork, beat me, and steal my well-deserved spot. How many walk-ons would Wetmore add? There wasn't a fixed number, but smart money said one. Maybe two? My family had driven from Iowa through the night to make the nine a.m. start time. I was completely taken aback that they had come, touched by the gesture, and more nervous than ever.

Approximately fifty men lined up for the start in an open field. The gun fired and I took off like a carefree child, bursting with pent-up energy, foolishly wasting it in the first mile, and saving nothing for the rest of the race. I was nowhere near the front. I had never begun a race so fast and been so far in the back. A number of my competitors surged ahead while others faltered behind me. The gap between us lengthened and I got stuck running by myself in no-man's land. By the time I hit the second mile, my lungs felt like someone had dumped a bottle of bleach down them. I inched up Jaw Bone Hill's steep rutted incline near the four-mile marker and pressed on, passing a few people, and then a few more. That, and *not* the lingering pain and discomfort, was the fun part of racing. I found a rare pleasure in pushing my body long after my mind had yelled "STOP!" Wobbling down the homestretch in survivor mode, trying to hold myself together, I crossed the finish line and looked to see where the others had finished. A tight pack of Colorado runners, including the Torreses and Ritzenhein, had run the time trial as practice. They had finished more than a minute ahead of me. Travis, decked out in a camouflage cut-off shirt and eye-concealing Oakleys, had slaughtered me. He was a shoo-in for the team. I had done what I needed to do: beat the other walk-ons and put myself into contention. Had I impressed Wetmore?

When I left the chute, my family was waiting off to the side. My aunt, cousins, and a few family friends were there too, representing a far larger group of fans than the ones gathered there in support of any other athlete. I noticed my mother pointing her camera, trying to capture the moment. I found my "Legends of the Fall" T-shirt in a clothes pile on the ground. Initially, I had refused to wear my "Legends" shirt in Nike-sponsored Buffalo country. That had changed after my first day at Potts when I noticed Jorge, Ed, and Dathan put on their high school team shirts after our run. As I wandered down to my family, stationed near the results page taped to the side of the team's white passenger van, Coach Wetmore intercepted me. He spoke from behind his sunglasses, "Matt McCue..."

I swallowed hard.

"I've spoken with the team and we've decided we want you to become a member of the Buffaloes. Would you like to join us?" Wetmore's tone would have been perfectly appropriate for firing someone.

Just like that, I was in! It made the physical suffering that had preceded it—every twinge and ache and burn—worth it.

"Yes! Thank you! Thank you, Coach Wetmore!" I stammered, unsuccessfully trying to match his impassive demeanor and quickly breaking out in a huge, unabashed grin. Yes! I had fantasized about this moment ever since I arrived in Colorado, practically experiencing it in my mind before it had actually happened. That did nothing to diffuse my excitement. I wanted to reach out and hug Coach Wetmore, to yell and scream and howl at the top of my lungs, to pump my fists in the air and let my emotions escape into the deep blue sky. Eighteen-year-old men are too young to achieve such a big dream. Thanks to Coach Wetmore, I had done it. I owed him a huge debt of gratitude, but before I could express myself, he spoke up.

"Welcome to the team," he said. "Now, let's get to work."

Right over his shoulder, I spotted the Colorado guys starting their cool down. Instinctively, I ran their way, joining—rather than chasing after—them for the first time. It felt right.

Members of the Colorado cross country team: Ed Torres is third from the left, then me, then Jorge standing shirtless, and Travis behind him. Dathan, the future national champion and two-time Olympian, is on the far right.

That night, along with my parents and my younger siblings, I celebrated at The Cheesecake Factory with a decadent slice of sinfully-rich peanut butter swirl cheesecake. Thanks to my high mileage and fast metabolism, the calories would burn off in my sleep. Afterwards, my family dropped me off at the steps of my dorm. Before they set off on the endless drive back to Iowa, my mother handed me a white envelope. I guessed it contained a few bucks. It did, along with a handwritten letter. On the brink of my first official Colorado practice, I read my mother's thoughts:

In the end, when you strip away all of it, I just want you to be happy. After I read Running with the Buffaloes, *which was dog-eared, because YOU had read it three times already, I knew you were hooked. Wetmore and CU to a runner like you... pure heroin. The ultimate high.*

While your father and I tried to focus on the academic side of your college search, in my heart, I knew it was just a sham. You wanted to run D1. The best in the land. CU. I couldn't argue with your choice: an idyllic beautiful spot, a hip young fun city, an Honors program that could pare down the #'s in your classes. All good.

What did I feel when you left for a summer in Colorado? Fear? I was afraid that if you didn't make the team, the disappointment would do one of two things: either send you spiraling into a despair and funk that would color your entire college experience OR send you into an obsessive frenzy that would fuel an entire year of manic training as you hoped to achieve the ultimate prize, a spot on Wetmore's elite team one year later. . .

I felt a giant knot of anxiety at the time trial. This enigma, Wetmore, the ponytailed guru hiding behind dark glasses and an abominable chamois shirt covered with buffaloes...hard to read, hard to know...and I was trying mightily to have the right posture, taking photos, but not too many. Cheering, but not too loudly. Never knowing where the line was. Feeling absolutely euphoric after you sauntered over and said, "I made it" and celebrating and just embracing the moment.

In my heart, it doesn't matter to me if you become an All-American or make it on scholarship or even run on the national championship team. I just want you to be able to look back and say, I took the path I chose and now I know. . .

My mother and I captured at the town park in front
of the Flatirons rising in the background.

III. AND IT BEGINS…

Freshman Year

I. A rare compliment: September 2001

Sunday morning Colorado practices were the price of admission. "Sunday runs" started promptly at eight, demanding that we, the envy of the collegiate distance running world, drag ourselves from our warm beds to hammer between fifteen and twenty miles. Lucky us, right? The runs took anywhere from ninety minutes to more than two hours for the mileage-monsters. Every Sunday run began at the "Buffalo", the life-sized gold statue right outside of the football stadium. After hearing Wetmore announce, "Time to get to work," the team would head for the white passenger van or individual cars. Collectively, the motorcade sped out of town and the fun began.

The morning following the time trial, I woke up at six-thirty, unable to fall back asleep. For the next hour, I paced up and down my dorm's empty halls, repeating a cycle of touching my toes, drinking water, and going to the bathroom. By seven-thirty, I couldn't stand being cooped up any longer, and headed over to the Buffalo. Travis was the only other person there. Too anxious to sit, we used each other's shoulder to balance as we stretched our quad muscles. Dressed in ratty black running shorts and a gym shirt, Coach Wetmore walked past at a quarter of eight and eyed us. "What are you two doing here?" he asked with a half-smirk, "You're erroneously early!"

Erroneously early! What a compliment!

Ten minutes later, when the men's and women's teams, about thirty runners in all, had gathered, we passed around the day's work-out document that Wetmore had marked with our mileage assignments. "Documents"—Wetmore's fancy name for pieces of 8.5 x 11 inch paper—were pinned daily to the bulletin board outside of the coaches' offices. They would write the story of my life over the next four years, instructing me on how far to run, what gear to pick up, and where I should travel to race. Wetmore's primary platform of communication was the first place every athlete went to at practice.

Magnolia Road. Those words stood out like searing black grill marks on the lined white paper that first Sunday morning. Eager to gulp down fifteen miles before breakfast, I expected the run to be one of the most pleasurable experiences of my life even if it assured a world of pulsing, wrecking-ball misery. Despite my walk-on dream, I had never given serious thought to what life on the team would be like. Hanging with my new teammates, I wondered, "Where do I go from here?" Easy. I hoped to rise from blue-collar walk-on to running on a national championship-winning team. Magnolia Road was the best starting point.

2.   I'm Matt McCue: September 2001

Christmas. That's what Jorge and Ed called equipment day. I had heard stories about our Nike sponsorship; the lowdown was that Santa and his elves had nothing on it. No longer would I have to dig for frayed hand-me-downs from the depths of a dusty laundry bin. I imagined myself walking away with brand new Air Maxes, the shoes my parents had always considered too expensive. I'd also receive every other conceivable piece of gear from black warm-up slicks embossed with a gold "Colorado" across the chest to running shorts, T-shirts, and gym bags, all the way down to ankle socks. Jorge and Ed had accumulated so many free clothes over the past two years that their stocked attic looked like the Colorado outlet of Niketown. I'm sure Dathan felt the same as the Torreses. Months ago, when he had qualified to represent the United States at a race in Europe, he had received a box full of Team USA clothes. I figured picking up Colorado sweats couldn't be as big a deal for them as it was for me.

The four of us rode the elevator down to the equipment room located on the sub-basement floor of Dal Ward. I had expected the room to look like a stocked concession stand where I simply had to point to whatever I wanted. In reality, it looked more like a jail cell. A white metal grate guarded the top of the window slot and the bottom opened wide enough to pass a shoebox through. Behind it, a row of black Colorado skiing jackets hung on plastic hangers. A stack of recognizable burnt-orange and brown Nike boxes shot from the floor like a skyscraper. The gatekeeper was a college student armed with a clipboard.

Jorge and Ed went first and gathered their presents. Dathan's armload rivaled that of the twins. Then I approached. "I'm Matt McCue."

The young man scanned his clipboard, checked my name, and handed me a pile half the size of what the other three had carried away. I waited for the rest, but nothing else came, not even my jersey. I wanted to ask the others why they had been given a set of clothes that was different from mine. I realized they were faster, but weren't we all on the same team? But my gut told me to keep quiet, to be thankful for what I held in my arms. Still, I felt that something wasn't quite right. Very quickly, I would learn that running in college was going to be quite different from what I was used to. Equipment day would be my first lesson. Fast or marginally slower, we were all on the same team. But, sometimes, it didn't feel that way.

3. Across the frosty grass: September 2001

Early one Friday morning, during my first month on the team, I pushed my shoulder into the heavy backdoor of my dorm, shoving it open. The late September air carrying the first breaths of a Rocky Mountain winter nipped at my gloveless fingers. Greeting the darkness was never easy, no matter how often I had done it. I took the first of many steps and left the dimly lit courtyard. Behind me, the crescent moon hung over the mountains.

Twenty minutes of jogging, ten minutes of calisthenics, a few strides, and one quick bathroom stop—I'd soon be fully awake and bounding into the workout. The team had to be "psyched and spiked" by six-thirty: practice beckoned. As my eyes adjusted, I ran on instinct, my legs talking to each other without me knowing what they were saying. Each foot strike hit the unseen sidewalk without hesitation. At Colorado, we only had one early-morning practice per week, on Fridays. The biggest difference between these sessions and my old Regina practices was that everyone warmed up together at Regina to the "church and back". The Colorado team warmed up alone before uniting on the starting line, only to separate into individually-tapered, Wetmore-assigned groups, once the workout started.

As I approached our temporary practice site, a campus field, the silhouettes of my teammates emerged from the darkness, each man thinking his own thoughts. I stopped at the knotted tree at one end of the field where everyone changed into their lightweight flats. Across the grass, Wetmore pushed a neon-orange click wheel around an imaginary oval to measure our loop. He scattered our discarded long-sleeved shirts on the ground to mark the circle's perimeter amid a surreal setting. The sun rose in the east and the moon dropped to the west. Hardened legs and sculpted calves strode across the crunchy, frosty grass. A coach swaddled in gray sweats cracked the workout whip with one hand and patiently readied his stopwatch with the other. In the background, the ghostly campus remained oblivious to the aspiring national champions in its midst.

Some of my teammates cracked jokes to keep the jitters at bay. An edgy smile here, a tense grin there. Nothing penetrated the seriousness that lay beneath my grave expression. The confidence I had carried over from high school had begun to wane, the result of getting my butt kicked on a daily basis. While I ran faster than ever before, I had finished near the back of the pack in every workout thus far. I knew I would have to get used to not always running in the front, but no amount of planning could have prepared me for the mental shock of watching my varsity teammates smoothly forge ahead. Still, nothing stopped me from pushing myself on every interval to try and hang with them. As a result, I found myself tossing the important ideas of rest and recovery out the window. Not only was I running every day, I was also running *hard* every day. I quickly slid back into my "one-year plan" approach. It had taken me four years to grasp patience at Regina, but once the Colorado practices started, and the allure of a championship became real, I forgot all of the lessons I had learned.

4. To be serious is the greatest joy: October 2001

After five weeks on the team and less than twenty-four hours before our first race, a document directed the walk-ons to Wetmore's office. He sat behind his desk, busily devising strategy on another document. We both knew why I was there. He pointed to the cardboard box on the floor and said, "They're in there." I picked up my brand-new Colorado jersey that was rolled into a ball and snugly wrapped with a rubber band. I immediately tried it on in front of a mirror in the bathroom. The stretchy fabric fit perfectly, molding itself to my chest rather than tugging at my shoulders like my old Regina jerseys. I now looked the part. Thus far, I had watched Wetmore spend the majority of his time at practice talking to the best runners, the same guys who received their jerseys along with the full set of gear on equipment day. Watching the investment being made in them had left me wondering about my place at Colorado. My uniform, Wetmore's blessing, gave me a better sense of where I stood.

The next day, I finished ninth on the team at our season-opener, the Rocky Mountain Shootout. It was a solid performance for a newcomer, and I straddled the line between the "B" team and the varsity team. Soon, I would learn where I would travel for the next meet.

After the race, my parents and I drove to a Boulder park. We walked away from the crowds and the kids zipping down the shiny slide toward an open grass field where I stripped off my black Colorado cross country T-shirt. Underneath, I wore my jersey. I had kept it on after the race, even though it had begun to stink from my dried sweat. I asked my mother to shoot half a roll of pictures for the scrapbook. I felt proud of myself and wanted something to immortalize the feeling so it wouldn't fade away. The long pursuit I had undertaken and the sense of fulfillment it had culminated in now made me feel even more privileged to be part of the tradition spelled out in the letters printed across my chest.

As my mother pointed her camera at me, I leaned against a tiny sapling and faced her. My hands fell to the side, hanging at my hips as though I didn't know what to do with them. Actually, I didn't. I had never smiled for my Regina team pictures. In fact, none of the boys had, in conformity with some unspoken reason no one could quite remember. We shot hard looks at the camera like rogue characters in a movie. Wearing my Colorado jersey, I tried the very same approach, but failed, landing in a gray area that was somewhere between a full-fledged grin and a cold stare. I looked like a young man at a crossroads, filled with excitement and wonder at the prospect of embarking on the path I had chosen for myself. My mother sent the photos to me weeks later. I hid them in the bottom of my desk drawer.

A few days later, I bumped into Travis in front of Balch Fieldhouse. I found it ironic that we had become friends. I had originally marked him as my walk-on rival. He had marked me as the same. But starting with that "erroneously early" Sunday morning, our comradeship had rapidly evolved. Like me, hard work had been Travis's trump card. We were two blue-collar walk-ons amid a team full of household names. Since the Colorado workout document listed the names from the fastest to the slowest, McCue would have been alone near the bottom without Macy. When we realized we needed an ally on the team, each had looked to the other to fill that role.

We had wandered over to Wetmore's office to learn where we would travel for our second meet: Greenville, South Carolina, or Fort Hays, Kansas. The team's top eight or nine runners flew to the big pre-nationals meet in Greenville, a mid-season "practice" for the real national championships five weeks later. Each team could race up to fifteen runners at the pre-nationals, splitting their squad between two races. The top seven ran in the varsity race and the remaining eight could compete in a second "open" race. Most teams sent fifteen runners. Colorado didn't, due to budget constraints. Our "B" team rode in the passenger van to Fort Hays. I had beaten Travis at the Shootout and had my sights set on

Greenville, but Wetmore had the final say. The consensus among my varsity teammates was that Fort Hays was for amateur athletes.

"How's it going?" asked Travis, a buckled cycling helmet covering his head. His bike was yards away and chained to the rack. He had just spoken with Wetmore.

"Good, man. You?" I asked.

"I'm good. Just talked to Wetmore and guess what?"

"What?"

"You're going to pre-nats!"

"And you are too?" I asked.

"Nope, just you. I'm stoked for you, buddy!"

"Oh man, I'm sorry to hear you're not coming with us. Are you pissed?" I asked.

"Nope, just psyched for you. Well, gotta go to class, but good job, man. Later."

As Travis pedaled away, I wondered about "Sunshine", the nickname the team had given him. Given that he was traveling to Fort Hays, how could he be so genuinely happy for me?

Two days before the team flew to Greenville, I walked into Wetmore's office, hoping to ask for a coveted pair of black Colorado warm-ups. On equipment day, I was given a pair of baggy gray sweatpants that looked like the kind my classmates wore to eight a.m. lectures. I was thankful for sweatpants, but they left me wanting more—to look like my teammates. Midday, between classes, I found Wetmore behind his desk, creating the day's workout document: ten 300-meter sprints with a fleeting one-minute rest between each. To the left of his desk, the wall-mounted shelves were filled with framed pictures of former athletes and thick training manuals. The flagstone wall behind his desk looked like it belonged in a chalet in Aspen. It was out of place in his tiny windowless nook, crammed under a low ceiling that occasionally rumbled with noise from the pounding feet of the university dance classes held upstairs.

In his office, Wetmore displayed the quote, "*Res severa verum gaudia,*" from Gustav Mahler, an Austrian symphony composer and conductor. It meant, "To be serious is the greatest joy." A philosopher from a different era, Wetmore hardly seemed like the kind of man who had to look to others for wisdom and inspiration. His encyclopedic brain was a fountain of knowledge, because he had once set himself the goal of reading every book in the world. While he had obviously failed to fulfill this impossible objective, he had built up a repertoire of pocket phrases from the masterpieces he did complete. I greatly respected his intellect.

His runners referred to him as "Wetmore" among themselves, but we never directly addressed him by his last name. It was either "Coach Wetmore" or "Mark". I felt "Coach Wetmore" was too formal and called him Mark.

"Hey, Mark!" I now said, "I was wondering, since I am going to pre-nats and all, is there any way I could get a pair of black warm-ups? Like the other guys?"

"Didn't we sign you up for a pair of gray ones?"

"Yeah you did—thanks, they're great, I really appreciate it. But I was just wondering if—since I'm traveling and all, and pre-nationals is a big meet—the black and gold ones, maybe I could..."

Wetmore stared at me, not expecting an answer to his rhetorical question.

When he didn't reply, I nodded. "You're right, the gray ones work fine, but I just thought—you're right, the gray ones work. Thanks."

I backed out, leaving the office within three minutes of my entry, as Mark returned to his workout document. Unsettled,

I walked to class, wondering what else I needed to do to be treated on par with the varsity guys. Hadn't I proved myself all summer and at the Shootout? And would it have killed Wetmore to give me a little advice instead of dismissing me so peremptorily?

At practice that afternoon with Jorge and Ed, I casually mentioned my confusion over Mark's refusal to issue me a pair of CU warm-ups. The next day, the twins came to my rescue with an extra pair of their own that they had found in their closets. I felt indebted to the five-foot six twins, even if their "small" size pants tightly hugged my thighs and ended way above my ankles.

5. That's why we do this—to run fast: October 2001

After my performance at the pre-nationals, I would wonder if I deserved to wear a pair of black slicks, borrowed or not. I had moved up from ninth to eighth on the team. But neither my teammate, who ran in the "open" race with me, nor I had a particularly strong showing. By my standards, that meant neither of us had won. I quickly discovered how much better Division I college athletes were than small-town Iowa runners. Collegians never seemed to slow down. On paper, the difference between high school's three-point one-mile races and college's five-miles didn't seem like much, but after lactic acid had bullied its way into my muscles, the two additional miles made my long legs feel like they were filled with sand. Our varsity team, the top seven, had distanced themselves from me, leaving me no chance to make the jump to it. In one month, they would run at nationals, but my season was, essentially, done. Since I had committed myself to the time trial six weeks ago, my physical peak had passed and my body had started to unravel. This wasn't unusual. Almost every freshman runner experienced it. It was necessary, like a rite of passage. To see how far I could push myself, I needed to find my breaking point. Fortunately, I wouldn't be beset by injuries, but running more than ten miles a day made me feel like I was one of the walking dead.

The week following pre-nationals, Wetmore gathered the entire team in the middle of the shadowy field house for our first serious talk. Document in hand, he sank into a folding chair, looking like a man at peace with himself. Never one to shout above a crowd, he waited for the team to meander over from the stretching circle and listen. He wouldn't bark, "Listen up!" to grab our attention. Instead, someone always had to slap the shoulder of the loud teammate next to him and cast his eyes toward our silently waiting coach, hinting that it was time to be quiet. Soon, the voices would die down to two...then one...then silence. All eyes were on him.

Before Wetmore started his speech, he would grouchily announce, "I hate giving speeches." It was ironic, he was a mesmerizing orator. He had the unique ability to fire people up without raising his voice. Self-deprecating, he joked about how he no longer understood what collegians considered cool. The team was charmed by the coach's dry wit, his special brand of humor. The only person who didn't join in the laughter was Wetmore himself. I have never figured out why.

I clearly remember his first speech. I had never heard anything like it before. As we sat in front of him, our outstretched legs resting on the rubber surface, Wetmore had leaned forward in his chair, rested his elbows on his knees, and explained how his team worked. "We have more than thirty of you here," he had begun, "and if I sat down to talk with each of you every day for three minutes, that would add up to almost two hours of my time and I don't have that kind of time in my day for everyone.

"You need to understand that I am going to give the majority of my time to those who run on varsity or are challenging for the national championships. The upcoming national championships are important. That's why we do this—to run fast. I have to take each of you into account in terms of how fast you run. However, I arrive at my office around nine every morning. My door is open."

Finally! Wetmore preached what I had hoped to hear for years: The fastest runners would be treated differently. Better. The only problem: I was far from the front.

6. "Gooooo, Buffaloes! YEAH!!": November 2001

On the third Monday in November, Travis and I skipped our classes to road trip nearly 2,000 miles across the country from Boulder to Furman University in Greenville, home to the 2001 NCAA Cross Country National Championships. Seven of our teammates had the chance to end the day as National Champions. We had to support them.

On Furman's campus-bordering golf course, a white-lined racecourse snaked over the lush Bermuda grass through the eighteen holes, finishing with one team capturing the glory. Today defined the season for the nearly 250 lithe runners who charged into their 10k race while fans of every shape and size and school loyalty flocked to the fairways and cheered.

"Gooooo, Buffaloes! Come on, Colorado! YEAH!!" Travis was going ballistic, roaring as if his words could somehow make a difference in the outcome. If his enthusiasm wasn't already obvious, his wardrobe removed all doubt. He wore his full Colorado uniform, gallivanting around the course in shorts that made a Speedo look baggy. (For good measure, he also wore a white bandana tied around his head like a pirate.) I had the same problem with my uniform shorts, which was why I never wore them anywhere but at a race. For the longest time, Travis and I hadn't been able to figure out why our shorts were much more "vacuum-packed" than our teammates'. Halfway through the season, we had noticed the slit in the side of them that ran high up our thighs closely resembled the women's style. It finally made sense. We had been issued women's uniform shorts, scaled to fit a waist the size of my wrist! Travis and I had no idea why. After my unsuccessful attempt to obtain the black slicks, I didn't dare try to exchange my hip-hugging pair. Running in the rarified air of Colorado demanded making sacrifices. If showing a little leg was one of mine, so be it.

Travis and I watched the gasping racers kick toward the finish. Their cheeks inflamed with exhaustion, perspiration dripping from their chins, their faces wreathed in grimaces, they spilled out of the chute, looking for their teammates and coaches, for someone to either celebrate or condole with. Walking back to the Colorado camp minutes later, Travis and I heard the howls before we could recognize their sources. Primal sounds blending exhaustion with jubilation, they came from our teammates, signifying a hard-fought victory. The lit scoreboard said "Stanford 91" and "Colorado 90". Lowest score won. We were National Champions by one point!

My seven teammates cheered, arms flung over their heads in joy. Sweaty hugs were exchanged. The exhaustion quickly evaporated from their legs. The physical suffering had been worth it. Journalists with notepads rushed over, followed by the lone cameraman and television reporter. Onlookers gathered, curiously observing the latest kings of collegiate cross country running. High school students dressed in their matching team shirts talked among themselves and pointed, "They're the Torreses. There's 'Ritz'. What do you think they eat?" Travis bounded past the crowd and greeted the team with high fives. When he tried to slap Wetmore's hand, the coach settled for a handshake.

Given that he had just won his first men's championship, Wetmore looked relatively subdued, smiling politely, but not as much as I remember Coach Brown had after our state championships. Brown had hugged us as if he would never see us again. Wetmore wasn't a hugger, but he liked to win as much as anyone else.

Unclear about my position in the celebration, I hung off to the side and offered my hand in congratulations whenever any of my teammates stepped back from their tight pack in the middle of the crowd. When Wetmore pulled the racers into the fairway to speak to them in private, Travis and I stayed with the fans in the rough. We were the only Colorado runners in attendance who hadn't competed. "Wasn't that something?" Travis asked. "Man, the guys ran great! Just great! Isn't this awesome? Three months on the team and we're national champions! This is awesome!"

"Yeah," I said, expelling a big sigh, smiling like everyone around me. As Coach Wetmore and the seven runners stood together in the distance, I silently considered the words echoing in my mind: "I have to look at each of you in terms of how fast you run." When I had congratulated Wetmore on the team's victory, how did he see me? As the guy who loved being part of the team so much that he traveled 2,000 miles across the country just to watch a thirty-minute race? Did he see me as the runner I was training to be? Or only by what the clock said? On a team where speed defined a person, I was unaware of my place. Technically, I was on a national champion team, but I had contributed nothing to the effort. I thought about joining the frenzy, maybe catching Wetmore's eye, offering a small nod, a hint of recognition, letting him know that even though I hadn't competed at nationals, I was as dedicated as anyone else. I remained a spectator on the fringes, watching and wondering. When the coach and my teammates joined the large crowd, the most genuine guy on the team, Travis "Sunshine" Macy, added a howl of his own.

7. "*Matt* McCue, I'm glad to see you here": December 2001

Christmas break. Returning to Iowa for the first time since I had left in the summer, I drove across town to Gleason Avenue where Coach Brown's modest two-story split-level blended in with every other home on the block. As a result, I had often rung the wrong doorbell.

"*Matt* McCue," Coach Brown greeted me, his trademark emphasis on the first syllable of a person's name intact, "I'm glad to see you here." He accepted the tin of cookies my mother had sent with me, and wrapped me in a hug, his hold still crushingly tight. I wasn't the first former athlete who had stopped by during the holidays. He had a constant flow of former runners visiting him. I was one of the many who had a standing invitation to his home.

Darlene cooked dinner in the kitchen upstairs and the aroma of pot roast wafted through the cozy house. I followed Coach Brown down five steps to his basement. Family pictures covered the walls of the narrow space. A brightly lit Christmas tree sat in one corner. The presents underneath were wrapped for his children and grandchildren. A History Channel special about the military aired on the house's sole TV.

As he relaxed in his La-z-Boy, I sat on the couch, and we talked for more than an hour. Actually, I did most of the talking, sharing every aspect of running at Colorado. When I finished, Coach Brown asked, "What do you think of the coach? Does he treat you well?"

I paused. No one had ever asked me that question. Wetmore possessed the coaching characteristics I yearned for, like the uncanny ability to craft workouts perfectly suited to help my body develop into that of a fast runner's. Without Wetmore, I was simply Matt McCue. With him, I had clout. I was Matt McCue, Colorado

Buffalo. Did he treat me well? The acclaimed coach treated me in accordance with how fast I ran: fairly, justly, and like a freshman walk-on. It's what I expected and accepted.

"Yes," I answered, "He treats me well."

Before we went upstairs for dinner, Coach Brown led me behind the La-Z-Boy to his windowless guest bedroom that was too cluttered to ever house any guests. Only slightly bigger than the single bed that lined the far wall, the "Trophy Room" looked like the Regina running museum. The bookshelves were crowded with team medals. Looking closely, I spotted a few Iowa *Coach of the Year* plaques inconspicuously lying on the wooden table. The notebook-sized team pictures were neatly arranged in a stack on the lower half of the bed. The top print showed runners in blue and yellow warm-ups and haircuts straight out of the '80s. Their faces beamed. When I picked up the team photo from my freshman year, Coach Brown gently rested his hand on my back, between my shoulder blades, and said, "Can you believe so many people have contributed to the tradition? Every runner who's ever worn a Regina jersey has contributed something to this room. It's kind of neat and I'm glad you're a part of it too."

Yes, high school had been neat, but thankfully, I had moved on to Colorado. As I surveyed the room, I saw faded memories. On my new team—which had just won the *National* Championship—practically *everyone* had gold state meet medals.

A few minutes later, we parted with an exchange of "Merry Christmas!" and an embrace.

"Stay in touch," he said. While I always heard out Coach Brown, sometimes, I didn't listen to him. Not surprisingly, this would be one of those times.

• • •

The 2001 National Championship trophy arrived at Dal Ward after my return to Boulder. The wooden, gold-encrusted prize sparkled from behind its protective glass like a priceless piece of art. The accompanying photo featured the seven national champions and the remaining team members, all dressed in matching black and gold warm ups, two rows aligned as one. (Only Wetmore was absent. He wasn't a smile-for-the-camera kind of guy.) Despite all my angst over my place on the team, I was there in the back row. Why then, did I see myself as an outsider, whenever I walked past the trophy case? I didn't have an answer. With many miles left to go, I focused on contributing to the proud tradition. To victory.

8.   Western outlaws at the O.K. Corral: April 2002

The bone-dry exhaustion that had been festering since the end of cross country season overtook my body in February. Determined to excel during outdoor track, I ignored the chronic fatigue, citing it as an occupational hazard of running with the best team in the land. I kept pushing myself long and hard. It was therefore no surprise to anyone but me when, during the spring season, my body crashed. The intensity of my training over the past eight months, including my efforts to keep up with Jorge, Ed, and Dathan on "easy" days, my practicing with the fervor that should have been reserved for races, and the draining Sunday runs had caught up with me at last.

I had my blood tested in April. Anemia, an energy-sapping iron deficiency, was the diagnosis. It explained the relentless exhaustion. In order to raise my depleted stores, I had to choke down a shot glass full of rust-colored (and rust-tasting) liquid iron twice a day. I could run "through" anemia without harming my body, but it would be months before I regained my strength.

That spring, while battling anemia and shot legs, I didn't think life could get much worse. Then Travis pulled up in front of my dorm one Saturday morning in his 1972 Toyota pick-up that was the same color as my liquid iron. Complete with a fiberglass topper over the bed and a shiny chrome skull on the gearshift, the truck looked like it should have been retired to the junkyard years ago. The bruiser croaked and choked whenever Travis shifted gears, leaving me worried it might unexpectedly grind to a dead stop on the highway. I used to think riding in Coach Brown's station wagon with its blue vinyl interior had to be the ultimate "roughing-it" experience, but this was far worse. Travis and I looked like Western outlaws on our way to the O.K. Corral.

Where could we be going in such a rig? Colorado Buffalo track meets.

Along with the other walk-ons, we traveled to a series of local competitions, proving grounds in places like Fort Collins and Greeley. If I ran an eye-catching race here, Wetmore might add my name to the out-of-state traveling roster for the next week, I figured. Since the varsity runners weren't required to attend the nearby meets, the coaches didn't shuttle a team bus or van. With his athletes competing almost every single weekend from January through June, I could understand why Mark wouldn't want to drive the lower, slower half of the squad to places like Greeley. He drove his own car, leaving people like Travis and me scrambling to find our own transportation. As a result, Travis became my Coach Brown. He often steered with his knees, while his hands, that were supposed to be on the wheel, expressed his unbridled enthusiasm over the book we had both just finished reading: *The Electric Acid Kool-Aid Test* by Tom Wolfe. We knew the story had heavily influenced Wetmore. That's why we had devoured it.

Unfortunately, freshman track season was a blur of poor races we wanted to forget. We were putting in the work all right, but something wasn't clicking.

After our final meet in Fort Collins, Travis and I searched for Wetmore, looking for some closure on our first year. It had been a grueling, continuous season, spread out over the last ten months from July to the end of April. We looked to our coach for much-needed advice and encouragement.

Travis and I found him on the track's backstretch where there were neither bleachers nor people; just the chain-link fence he leaned on. In front of us, the final few competitors were abandoning the infield. Athletes from Wyoming and South Dakota had already packed their bags and piled into their team vans. Dusk encroached on our territory, hastening Wetmore's already brief closing words. Travis and I stood on either side of him as he stared beyond the bare track, at what I couldn't fathom. He instructed us to take two weeks off from running before starting to train for cross country season, the heart of which was six long months away. Thankfully, Wetmore was already thinking about our next season. It meant we wouldn't be dopped from the team.

Two weeks later, in May, I packed my belongings into the back of Jorge and Ed's red Ford Explorer and left Sewall Hall. I was moving in for the next three years with my teenage heroes at the so-called "Fight Club". After athletic scholarships left them with extra money originally set aside by their parents for tuition, Jorge and Ed had invested in a mountain shack they found in shambles. It rested on a few acres of land five miles west of the campus and less than a quarter-mile down the road from Magnolia. They had hired a construction crew to tear down the old structure and build a new one in its place. Nestled in the rocks and pines of Boulder Canyon next to the flowing creek, the Taj Mahal of college pads was erected. It would eventually include a 64-inch TV, an eight-person hot tub with massage jets, and a pool table. *Sports Illustrated on Campus* featured the Fight Club in an article and encouraged MTV to use the log cabin to launch "The Real World: Boulder". When the twins asked me if I wanted to rent one of the five rooms, I resisted the urge to reply, "Yes, because I once considered you guys to be gods." All I said, instead, was, "Yes."

Life at the Fight Club, which Wetmore called the "country club", with Jorge, Ed, and Dathan, another recent addition, lifted my spirits. Since I had been accepted, it didn't even bother me that the "room" Jorge and Ed had rented out to me was a 6 x 6 foot storage closet sandwiched between the garage and the washing machine.

IV. THE "MAGIC" FORMULA
RUN A HUNDRED MILES A WEEK?

Sophomore Year

1. Mount Elbert: The most pleasurable $4.99 prime rib dinner of my life: July 2002

After one daybreak run during the summer between my freshman and sophomore years, a couple of the guys were hanging around at Potts, stretching and talking about how great it was to be able to train without having to worry about homework. Minutes later, Mark showed up and caught our attention by casually throwing out a seemingly off-the-cuff idea: run up Mount Elbert, the tallest mountain in Colorado and the second highest in the contiguous United States. Colorado had fifty-four "fourteeners," mountains exceeding 14,000 feet, and Mount Elbert reigned over them all, topping out at 14,440 feet. Wetmore, who would lead the trip, emphasized that the proposed run was completely voluntary. Travis and I figured that he would have another reason to keep us on the team if we nearly killed ourselves by scaling the peak. We were in.

On a Friday afternoon in late July, ten men, two women, and Wetmore endured the three-hour mountainous drive from Boulder to Mount Elbert, located ten miles south of Leadville in the San Isabel National Forest. If the Fight Club was nestled in the mountains, Mount Elbert's trailhead was remote, hidden away from civilization. A potholed dirt road welcomed us, once we had left the highway, and led us to the trailhead. In front of us, Mount Elbert seemed to bulge outward from the ground like Buddha's belly, giving it a wide girth that disguised its unparalleled height. Lacking the imposing shark-teeth features of the Flatirons we were used to, it didn't look particularly intimidating. Still, it begged to be climbed—or in our case, run.

We set up camp in the middle of an evergreen forest between the trailhead and a rushing stream. One of my new freshman teammates owned a four-person pop-up trailer that we had hauled up from Boulder. That's where the Torreses, Dathan, and I, along with a few others—eight people in all—planned to sleep. Wetmore had brought his tent and pitched it next to his Subaru, about 200 feet away from us. We didn't have much free time in the late afternoon, but Travis, Wetmore, and I managed to get in a little reading. The rest of the guys played cards.

That night, we drove into Leadville and ate dinner at a Mexican restaurant. As we inhaled baskets of chips and salsa, Mark outlined our ascent. Everyone would meet at the trailhead the next morning at seven. Breakfast and stretching needed to be taken care of beforehand on our own. He planned to split us into small groups based on our fitness level, staggering our start times, with the slower guys leaving first, followed by the faster groups, minutes later. Theoretically, everyone would arrive on top within a ten-minute window. Wetmore warned us not to run too hard. He didn't want someone sparking the slightest bit of inflammation that could spiral out of control and end in a season-wrecking injury. Run too hard? That was typically Wetmore. He knew that merely walking up Mount Elbert would leave us wheezing.

Now might be the appropriate time to ask the obvious: exactly *what* part of this sounded like summer vacation fun? Excellent question! Our lot was wired differently than most. We were young men who thrived on challenging ourselves—our limits. It was what made us feel alive.

That night, our group gathered around the campsite's wooden picnic table. Forcing fluids down our gullets and snacking on chocolate animal crackers dipped in peanut butter, we told rowdy stories, trying to outdo each other. An electric lantern provided a flicker of light as Wetmore shared his experiences of coaching his former New Jersey high school and club runners. Years ago, he had driven some of them out to Colorado for a summer running trip. In the spirit of gamesmanship, they had participated in "heart rate contests", where they had dashed up the peaks surrounding us to see who could push their pulse higher than the others. One year, the winner had apparently pressed so hard, he had begun coughing up "black stuff".

Thanks, Mark, I thought, that's exactly what we wanted to hear hours before our test. Camping in the wild felt very grassroots. No one seemed worried about mileage, split times, and national championships. As the night had drawn on, Wetmore's tangents gave way to grand stories where he laughed at the punchlines alongside us. He seemed to let his guard down and the coach-athlete barrier between us vanished. In a rare moment, Wetmore talked to us the way an old friend would have.

We bedded down for the night. The coach went off to his tent and our full camper divided the cramped sleeping quarters. Bundled in a jacket and stocking hat, Travis stuffed his sleeping bag under his arm and walked in the direction of the stream to sloom out in the open under the glittery Constellations burning bright. For those of us tucked safely in the pop-up trailer, his decision immediately notched up our respect for him. Mere millimeters of mesh netting protected us from roaming animals, but at least we had some sort of barrier. What about Travis? Fortunately, his stringy body wouldn't make for a hearty meal, if a bear or mountain lion decided to snack on him. Still, before we shut our eyes, we played the "picking game", laying claim to Travis's possessions, just in case. I called dibs on the chrome skull on his rusty truck's gearshift.

At seven sharp the next morning, everyone met at the trailhead. The anticipation of the day ahead seemed to beg for less enthusiasm and more solemnity. The weather, always a concern in the mountains, couldn't have been more idyllic. The sun and the moon shared space in the sky. All we could see was the deep blue ether of Colorado egging us on to "Have a day!" as Coach Brown used to cheer enthusiastically before big races.

Travis set out before me in a group that included his father who had driven the two hours from Denver that morning. Built like a sequoia, Travis's dad planned to bang his way up the mountain like the rest of us. Minutes later, my three-person pack clicked our watches. We left behind full water bottles, discarding them as superfluous weight. Foolish? Yes, especially for someone like me who had spent many nights out in the backcountry. But we wanted to feel as light on our feet as possible. Our reasoning made the decision seem practically foolproof. Mere steps later, the rocky trail turned steep, twisting through the tree line and taunting us with the challenge that lay ahead. The four-and-a-half-mile trek boasted an alarming incline of nearly 1,000 feet per mile and very little in the way of switchbacks. Each lumbering step seemed to confirm my suspicion that I was working real hard, but going nowhere.

When I caught up with Travis above the tree line, I found him laboring like me. Our heart rates were off the charts and still climbing: thump!thump!thump!thump!thump! The mountains were Travis's home and he wouldn't concede a single step to me. We continued together, the Colorado native and the flatlander from Iowa. Like everyone else, including Wetmore who was slogging up with us, we barely moved faster than a walk in the final half-mile, our efforts reduced to almost nothing by the thin air.

"Can—you—HUH!—believe—these—HUH!—views?" asked Travis, staring out into the expanse of snow-capped peaks in every direction.

My eyes remained locked on the talus-lined trail. "I—HUH!—don't care—I—HUH!—just want to—get—HUH!—to the—top!" I replied in pants, after coming across another false peak.

Groups of hikers carrying wooden trekking poles and expedition packs littered the side of the trail. They rested their oxygen-starved bodies and attempted to catch their breath—HUH!HUH!HUH!HUH!HUH!—as Travis and I scurried past on the single track.

After seventy-five minutes, we had reached the final 100 meters, a flat bed of rock disks. The smooth plane was the best welcome mat I could ever have hoped to find. Our group stood on the highest point in the state and shared sips from a water bottle Travis's dad had prudently snatched up and carried at the last minute. As the marshmallow clouds blew in, we started down. The urgency was gone. The descent would be relatively lazy and easy. We had gravity on our side.

Fifty-eight minutes later, we returned to our campsite where we finished the morning with a painfully cold, waist-deep ice bath in the glacial stream. That night, we went to a restaurant that advertised an early-bird special for only $4.99. I greedily consumed the most pleasurable prime rib, baked potato, and chocolate cake dinner of my life. Satiated, and ready for bed, we returned to our campsite. By eight, it was pitch black and silent outdoors. Travis chose to sleep out again next to the stream.

The following morning, Travis and I stretched—runners are constantly stretching *something*—on the shore of neighboring Turquoise Lake after a ten-miler around the water's edge. Our shoes and socks carelessly tossed to the side, we waited for Jorge, Dathan, and Ed to finish their twelve miles before returning to Boulder. Despite his grizzly summit push, Wetmore had chalked up his daily run. Travis and I found ourselves alone with him, giving us an opening to ask about the budget-cut rumors we had heard the week before from our teammates. We had quickly caught on that we would be among the first to go, if Wetmore thinned the roster. We were more than worried. The last week of uncertainty had been painful, the thought of leaving the Buffaloes inconceivable.

With enough sense to raise the matter right after we had run up the tallest mountain around, I started, "Mark, we've heard this budget-cut rumor," and Travis finished with, "Should it be something for us to worry about?"

Wetmore paused, looked down at his clasped hands, then crossed his arms and stared at the awe-inspiring views in every direction, weighing his thoughts. He looked off in the distance when he told us how much he valued our loyalty, strong work ethic, and commitment. The coach conceded that while he would have to be careful with the budget, he would find a way to keep us on the team.

Thank God, I exhaled. My anxiety finally subsided with Wetmore's reassurance.

2. Remember when you were at your best: August 2002/ March 2001

My biggest concern at Colorado had always been *making* the team, not *staying* on it. I often wondered: what more can I do? I was ticking off the miles, lifting weights, stretching, dipping into ice baths, eating right, and sleeping soundly. By virtue of committing so much time to my sport as well as going to bed so early, I had little to no social life. Any extra energy I had was invested in earning my degree—the reason I was in college! But, to me, racing fast was the priority. I felt ashamed of myself for *still* not climbing up the roster. I was doing all I could to improve, and the reality was that I had risen only far enough to ensure I would not be cut. A number of blue-chip recruits had recently joined the team. Wow, they had an explosive level of talent and had already beaten me, adding to my frustration. Afraid that Wetmore might perceive me as weak-willed, I refrained from confiding in him. Nor could I ask him for help.

But, after Mount Elbert, I decided I needed help, if I was going to succeed during my sophomore year. I wrestled with the thought of sharing my angst with Coach Brown, but after the way I had brazenly left him for the promise of Colorado, my pride wouldn't allow me to go crawling back to seek his advice. I decided not to call him.

However, a few days before cross country season officially kicked off, I escaped for a stress-free trail run on my own. The solitude offered me the chance to reflect on one of Brown's favorite truisms: "Remember when you were at your best and be there again." He had used that quote before the state meet to remind the team of their best races. It had worked for me before. Alone in the woods, I let my mind wander back to my senior year of high school, a Saturday morning in March 2001...

A month after Coach Brown had declared, "I'll let you run wild, but you have to run wild on my terms," he and I journeyed through our final track season together. In a surprising twist, our Saturday-morning workouts, where I ran and he rode his bike alongside, had become a welcome ritual for both of us.

Arriving at Regina a few minutes before nine, I pulled my fleece headband over my ball cap. It looked goofy, but it was cold and raining. Coach wouldn't laugh. A punctual "the-bus-leaves-on-my-watch" man, he drove into the vacant parking lot a minute later and pulled his blue Schwinn from the back of his jeep.

"Are we ready?" he asked amid the sheets of rain, the bike already dripping. His gray-blue eyes squinted against the drops, tiny lines stretching themselves out across his temples. Coach Brown wore a baby-blue rain slicker and matching waterproof pants. He looked like Papa Smurf.

"Let's go," I replied. The billowy clouds sat low as a piercing rain spewed from them. The streets were slick and black, empty of traffic. The aroma of bacon leaked from the houses, seducing the inhabitants into hibernating during the seemingly endless Iowa winter.

We separated when we hit the sidewalk, less than 100 meters into the twelve-mile run. I moved to the front; Coach Brown trailed a few steps behind. Neither of us uttered a word. With a companion to share the road, silence can be comforting.

We left the city and traveled toward the Iowa countryside. The concrete road ran in front of us like a river of gray. Spray pelted our faces when a passing truck bumped over a pothole. We were the only two people on the road, lost in a sea of red barns, wheat-colored fields, and rows of leafless trees waving their chocolate-hued branches.

Many times, we tried to talk, but for the majority of the journey, we yo-yoed. Either Coach Brown would fly down a hill and wait for me to catch up or I'd pull away on an uphill and he would try to rein me in. Our last climb was no exception, the only difference being that by then, it was snowing.

I never admitted it to him, but the way Coach had shared the road and pedaled next to me through blowing flakes made me feel like I was invincible. Wanting to feel like that again, I held onto the memory during the fall and continued working hard. I increased my mileage from seventy-five miles a week to eighty-five, including eighteen on Sunday morning, and built a strong foundation to run faster than I ever had in my life. The results didn't show immediately during the cross country season, but by spring, my confidence had returned. I would finally have the breakthrough I had been chasing.

3. Mother Nature, an unrelenting beast: March 2003

A breakthrough wouldn't have been nearly as fulfilling without having to overcome a few obstacles along the way. One unexpected challenge came in late March, courtesy of Mother Nature. An abominable snowwoman, she took her aggression out on Boulder in a pre-spring blizzard that clobbered the Front Range late one night. The violent storm forced the city to close icy Canyon Road, a rare occurrence that eliminated our only connection between the Fight Club and town.

Around eight-thirty the next morning, I woke to a dark house that felt like an ice box. The electricity lines were dead, knocked out by the snow's weight. When I couldn't hear the morning commute roaring past, I stayed under the covers. With the snowstorm literally upon us, most people trapped in the canyon probably figured there was no going anywhere that day.

An hour later, my roommates and I shuffled out of bed. Outside, we saw a solid field of thigh-high snow extending from the Fight Club's front door, engulfing the roundabout driveway and continuing down to Canyon Road 100 yards away. After dressing in every piece of winter-weather attire we owned, Dathan and I grabbed the only two shovels in the garage. Jorge and Ed settled on plastic rakes. Our neighbors brought over a snowblower and the eight of us relentlessly dug for the next two and a half hours. Finally, sweating from the unexpected chore, Jorge pulled us together. "It looks pretty good. Now we can at least get a car out."

"Jorge, the road is closed," Ed told him. "Where are we going to drive?"

He had a point.

The next logical step would have been to build a fire in the fireplace and boil a pot of hot cocoa over the open flame, drinking it in slowly as the gray smoke escaped from the chimney. But, freakishly, we had more important plans than indulging in liquid chocolate, if that's even possible. We robotically changed into tights, long sleeves, waterproof vests, caps and gloves. Mother Nature could stop a lot of things like electricity and cars. We wouldn't let her stop us. On Wednesdays, we were scheduled to run fifteen percent of our weekly quota. I had recently been experimenting with 100 miles a week; that meant fifteen for me, as well as for the others. It was an aggressive workload, where we walked a fine line between injury and victory.

Since snow covered the dirt trails, we used the lifeless Canyon Road which had been partially cleared. It would have been one of the busiest roads in Boulder on a normal workday. We jogged over the wooden bridge above the creek and clicked our watches. Like Coach Brown had said whenever the Iowa weather turned inclement, "Run tough when it's tough to run."

Even at midday, Boulder Canyon remained shrouded in white, from the heavy flakes and the low-hanging clouds. We cruised down the center of the road, atop the yellow lane-dividing line. It felt rebellious and freeing. Despite the massive orange snowplows that threatened to flatten us with each pass and the police roadblock set up at the bottom of the canyon, our Wednesday run into town proceeded smoothly. After forty-five minutes, we popped into Balch. Colorado's closed campus was devoid of life, yet we all knew at least one person would be there in his office: Wetmore.

Mark also lived up Boulder Canyon, but had driven down before the police erected their roadblock. Seemingly indifferent to the weather, he penned the day's assignments as if the sun shone and all was as usual. Almost the entire team would show up two hours later for practice, wearing the same "Snow? *What* snow?" attitude as Wetmore. By the time we ran to his office, we had completed half of our workout, so he waived our attendance at practice and sent us back home, knowing we'd complete our remaining seven and a half miles along the way. With vests, tights, and shoes covered in melting snow, our small group headed back into the storm. We ran on the Creek Path that had been cleared by pint-sized tractors. (The running path was one of Boulder's first transportation routes to be shoveled. We had expected nothing less.) After we had convinced the police that they had to let us past their barricade because "we live in the canyon!" and "yes, we know cars aren't allowed up the road. That's why we're going to run!" we started the last push.

We reached the Fight Club and continued past the ninety-five-minute mark, ultimately clocking in at two hours, about eighteen miles. The extra distance convinced us that no one in the world could be working harder than we were at that moment. But we might as well have kept going, we thought, because without electricity or running water, we didn't have much waiting for us back at the Fight Club. We did our best to improvise. That night, we cooked lasagna on the grill, melted snow for drinking water, and skipped showers. As darkness fell, we covered ourselves in layers of blankets, lit a cluster of candles, and listened to the Iraq War coverage on a battery-powered radio.

4. What was I doing here? April 2003

Rip! My first step out of bed felt like someone was engaged in target practice, with the muscle bellies of my calves serving as the bull's-eye. Rip! Rip! Rip! My legs were trashed, a result of the night before. I had run twenty-five laps around the rock-hard track in the Mount San Antonio College 10,000 meters in Walnut, California.

My delayed soreness was worth it. I had finally run a race that met
my high expectations. The California night had provided all of the
necessary elements for a fast distance race: no wind, a chill that saw
fans pulling on jackets, and rain that had stopped minutes before I
toed the line. I finished my 6.2-mile race in 30:38, a personal-best
time that had placed me in the middle of the varsity-caliber field.
In high school, I had barely been able to race at the same pace, 4:55
per mile, for a two-mile stretch. Running tough in Colorado's blizzard one month ago had paid off with a breakthrough. To cap off
the night, my dad had driven me along with a carload of my teammates, to an In-N-Out Burger. At midnight, scores of paper-thin
distance runners packed the famous burger joint, gorging on well-
deserved "double-doubles", the grease running down our chins.

Now on this Friday morning, my post-race workout consisted
of light jogging to alleviate the soreness in my tender calves followed
by a break-up-the-knots massage from the athletic trainer. Leaving
my hotel room, I made a beeline for the elevator, the thought of
using the stairs quite beyond me, even though I often ran 100 miles
per week.

The doors opened. Wetmore leaned against the back of the
empty car, hands firmly clasped behind his back. He wore running
shorts and a Nike T-shirt. I had not expected to see him. He had
not expected to see me either.

"Matt McCue," he said, as I entered.

"Good morning, Coach Wetmore." I nodded and got in, unin-
tentionally betraying the remains of a slight smile that hadn't left
my face since I finished my 10k.

"Matt McCue," he said again, his lips twisting into a fleeting
wry grin, my race evidently on his mind. "Thirty minutes today.
Easy. You've got 10,000 meters of racing in your legs; so let's be
careful. We don't want to get greedy."

I nodded. In Wetmorespeak, that meant I had done a good job. Ding! Before I could respond, the elevator doors had opened. We stepped out and walked through the lobby and the sliding doors. The semi-circular driveway offered two options, one to the left, the other to the right. Wetmore proceeded to the left; so I headed to the right and took that first jarring step against my leg muscle's wishes. Rip!

Like Mark, I had a nose for finding a route that would lead me away from the traffic and crowds. As I headed down a winding back road that separated green hills dotted with mansions, I reflected on my time so far at Colorado. I remembered Coach Wetmore's first piece of advice: it would take two years of uninterrupted training before I could see the efforts of my hard work. Post-race double cheeseburgers aside, I had lived the dedicated life. I was on the right track to better things.

Proudly competing in the Colorado uniform, my focused eyes
convey my thoughts.

5. Did you hear me cheering for you? April 2003/ April 2001

The week following Mount SAC, my mother sent me a picture with a sticky note glued to it that said, "We're proud of you." I knew she had left out, "No matter how you run, we'd still be proud of you." The picture of Coach Brown and me didn't contain any writing; yet, it said more.

As far as I had known, Coach always sat high above the track and watched the action from the last row of bleachers. A stopwatch hung from his neck; a dog-eared notebook of split times sat on his knee. His entourage of assistants—a sprint coach, a distance coach, and a burly throws coach, most of them his former athletes—surrounded him. Coach Brown made his annual foray to buy a funnel cake at the state meet, but for the most part, he remained seated, his gray-blue eyes alert. Paying homage, coaches from other schools would make a mid-meet pilgrimage to chat.

Brown's athletes also sought his validation. He had a natural ability to sift through the muck of every disappointing race and extract the positive. He wanted his athletes to check in with him after every race; so we often talked to him at least three or four times a night. Athletes on a quest, we carried our spikes, our lungs still burning. Coach Brown offered sage advice. He was a Catholic Dalai Lama, sitting, watching, waiting, and cheering, "Come on, *Matt* McCue!" That's why I found my mother's picture so intriguing. It contradicted everything I thought I knew.

She had snapped it two years ago during the high school boys' 3,200 meters at the Drake Relays, a track meet as famous in Iowa as In-N-Out Burger was in California. The four-day event drew professional and collegiate athletes from all over the world. The high school races, though, were limited to the top twenty-four Iowans. Like the Indiana basketball state tournament, the Drake

Relays brought together preps from both big and small schools, pitting them against each other to determine the state's best. Given Regina's modest size, Coach Brown liked to say we were "running with the big dogs", if we made it.

My senior year, I qualified, so one Thursday afternoon in late April, Coach and I drove to Des Moines in the school's fifteen-passenger van. He never played music in the school bus. But this time, he took charge of the radio, found the country music station, and let the program blare forth at a deafening level. On the two-hour trip, I listened to more country music than I had ever needed to. I even lay down in the back seat to fake a nap, thinking he would turn the music off. He did not.

We arrived at an empty 14,000-seat Drake Stadium, the same blue track that hosted the Iowa state track and field meet. By Saturday, Drake would awaken, and the gracious heartland fans would fill every seat for the thirty-ninth year in a row. My first race was held on Thursday night during the distance running carnival where the crowd was sparse. The photo caught me mid-race, my arms pulled back at my sides, my blue Regina jersey plastered to my chest with sweat. The lead pack ran in the foreground rounding the second turn. I was there, lost in a mob of red, black, and gold jerseys. First, I analyzed and critiqued my form. I looked strong. Then I checked out the crowd's reaction, my eyes drawn to one man, practically the only person in his section. Coach Brown. My mother hadn't intended it, but she had captured his raw emotion when he didn't know anyone else was looking. The only person in his row, he stood on the wooden bleacher. His eyes were focused on me. His hands were raised far above his head. His mouth was open. I had no idea what he was saying. My guess: "Come on, *Matt* McCue!"

Many times after a race, spectators would ask me, "Did you hear me cheering for you?" Though I would politely affirm, "Yes.

Thanks, it really helped," the truth was I rarely heard anyone. When the gun cracked, the outside world ceased to exist until I had crossed the finish line. Coach Brown never asked if I had heard him during my Drake Relays race. He never admitted he had cheered for me as if he were at a sold-out country-music concert, rather than in a deserted stadium. The picture said enough. And looking at it two years later in Colorado made me realize that Coach had cared for me more than I knew.

V. THE MOST SUCCESSFUL PERSON IN THE WORLD

Junior Year

1. Busted: May 2003

The news shocked me more than anyone else. In late May, right after we had finished our sophomore year, Travis told me he was leaving the team. His legs had broken down, trashed from the stress of logging taxing miles for two years. The free and fluid muscles of his quads and hamstrings and calves had congealed into one knotted mess that deep tissue massage couldn't untangle. Travis's slipping race results merely corroborated what the telltale signs had been indicating all along: his body had busted. In pursuit of a championship, he had run himself to exhaustion.

Travis had wrestled with the idea of leaving the team for three months, but had waited until the end of track season to make his final decision. I had watched as he tried desperately hard to get apparently nowhere. One day, the emotional toll had finally become too much and he had walked into Wetmore's office. After thanking Mark for giving him the opportunity to run with the Buffaloes, he had walked out and never looked back.

My ally had moved on.

Having looked forward to finishing our four years together, it saddened me to see Travis leave the team. Fortunately, our friendship had always extended beyond running. And one day, he would give me the kind of advice that would be invaluable in helping get me through my biggest individual challenge in college—one that I had never even anticipated.

2. An honorable run: June 2003

While Travis had left on his own terms, I still planned on leaving Colorado on mine—as a success. Weeks later, at the end of a hot summer day, I picked up my mail and did a double take at the sight of the first letter on the pile. The return address was from the University of Colorado. Handwritten above it was a single word: "Wetmore". It was my first—and, though I didn't know it then— my only letter from the coach.

I imagined the worst. My previous track season had rolled up and down like the undulations of Magnolia, the high point being my breakthrough at Mount SAC. The low came at the Big 12 Outdoor Championships 10K in Austin, Texas. I had hoped to earn All-Big 12 Conference Honors. On race day, I unexpectedly felt nauseous and barely ate or drank anything. Halfway through the night race in the South's oppressive heat and humidity, I began to feel so woozy I thought I might collapse. The vertigo led to cold chills, even though it was 85 degrees. Determined to cross the line, no matter what, I had finished near the back.

Now, running my hands over the smooth envelope, I speculated that Wetmore's letter would say simply, "Matt, it's time for you to move on." A week earlier, I had written him my annual post-season "Thank you" note. I prayed he had received it before he wrote this. After procrastinating endlessly, I finally tore open the envelope. Wetmore's scrawl danced across the Buffalo stationary:

Matt,

I often fear that it can be disappointing to stand on the edge of the spotlight of a Torres or Ritz. Remember that you train and live as seriously and committed as anyone and when it is time to move on, you'll know you had as honorable a run as anyone. Thanks for your great character.

Wow. Over the past two years, I had wondered how Wetmore felt about me. His words were unexpected, and appreciated. I read the letter many times, blown away that Mark said *I* lived as committed as anyone. But for all that it said, the letter left one big question unanswered: what defined an honorable run?

3. Sleeping in, reading the *Times* cover to cover: September 2003

As I began my junior year, Mark Wetmore remained nearly as enigmatic to me as he had the day I had met him. Whenever I thought I knew what made him tick, he would surprise me, the note being the latest example. I learned the most about him through my Sunday runs. My family had always attended Sunday-morning Mass, but that changed for me in Colorado. Wetmore didn't believe in a god, Christian or otherwise. Sunday mornings on Magnolia Road provided him his religious service. His daily runs gifted him a slice of heaven. For nearly thirty years, he had spent Sunday mornings with athletes. Before he left New Jersey for Colorado, Wetmore had met his Edge City Track Club and Bernardsville high school runners for long workouts on the never-ending stretches of city concrete. While men his age brunched with their families, Mark, who didn't believe in marriage and had no children, led us to Magnolia Road. And, at other times, to Coot Lake, the Grange or Gold Hill. Each eternal dirt route was a vital piece of our training puzzle.

Wetmore began Sunday runs with us. As we pressed ahead, he would tackle his usual sixty-minute workout with no concessions for his age or for the knife-like neuromas in his feet that he had been ignoring for years. The only cure for the pain was rest, something the coach hadn't indulged in since he had commenced his consecutive-day streak nearly thirty years ago. Finishing his Sunday run early, he'd wait in the front seat of his Subaru for the next hour as his teams completed their homework. Taut bodies trickled in at different intervals—the fifteen-milers and the seventeen-milers. No matter how often I spent more than two hours running to the twenty-mile benchmark, Wetmore would invariably be there upon my return. Only a handful of diehards would still be around, stretching their battered legs. I'd amble to the coach's driver's side window and poke my head inside the car.

"How was it?" he'd ask.

"Good," I'd reply, even if it hadn't been.

That was it. Wetmore knew I had traveled twenty miles on foot. I knew he had waited for me. The rest went unspoken.

The lore associated with Mark's Sunday runs wouldn't have been nearly as mythic without Magnolia. The road had no equal, and that was both a blessing and a curse. An intoxicating challenge, it offered runners who believed they were tough the ultimate test. "Magnolia doesn't lie," affirmed Wetmore, pointing out that the rutted road, rather than he himself, had the last word in assessing fitness.

What had motivated him to continue rising early on Sunday mornings and meeting his runners? After one Magnolia run, I had heard him pose the same question to a small group of us. He had sheepishly admitted that sleeping in and reading *The New York Times* cover to cover in bed sounded appealing. Would it ever happen? I didn't believe so. Sunday runs were—and are—in Wetmore's blood, as much a part of him as the legs he runs on.

Coach Wetmore, on the far right, checking his watch and keeping tabs on me, the third runner from the left, during a race at the Buffalo Range.

4. Salt-crusted shorts beneath a ribbed torso: October 2003

"Magnolia doesn't lie." Those words were much easier to hear when, one Sunday in the fall, I had powered through two hours up there and my legs had felt weightless the entire way, a sign that I was ready to race fast. Six days later, at the pre-nationals race, I ran a time that proved I was good enough to be a varsity contributor on almost every Division I team in the nation. One team where I seemed to fall short was my own, a trade-off for competing for Colorado that I had willingly accepted. Thankfully, the hunter, not the hunted, I was rounding into form with five weeks remaining in our cross country season.

I walked into practice the following Monday, ready to take, in Wetmore's words, "the next logical step". The workout document said: eighty-five minutes—about fourteen miles—"steady". Steady meant a medium pace, roughly six minutes per mile for us. No one questioned Wetmore. If he had asked me to run across the country, I would have laced up my shoes.

When my teammates opened the field house doors, I sat right off the frontrunners' shoulders. While most of them had recently beaten me at the pre-nationals, Magnolia told me I was on the brink of competing for a spot where I had always envisioned my-self: the front. My plan changed three steps out the door, when the pace flew out of control with surge after surge. Five guys battled each other. None were willing to back down. Our trailing pack of eight followed closely. Everyone believed they were indestructible; so there was no hesitation in our response. Go!

It was another day in the life of a Buffalo.

My face quickly turned the color of tomato juice. My upper body felt like it was strapped in a straightjacket, even though my arms pumped furiously. Studying my teammates' inscrutable body language and poker faces, you wouldn't have been able to gage if any one of them was already suffering the way I was. I suspected most were; the deep and heavy breathing hinted at it.

Wetmore called the run "Fourth Street", named for the road where we claimed the majority of our miles. Our route carried us along the Boulder Creek path and over the cement waves that rolled through Fourth Street's residential neighborhood. Near the halfway point of the out-and-back run, we would meet the dirt floor of the Wonderland Lake trail, thereby obtaining some relief for our legs from the bone-breaking hardness of concrete.

At mile two, I realized that if I continued pushing at that speed instead of pacing myself, the results could potentially be disastrous. Hard work was my saving grace, but even hard work had its breaking point. I didn't want to drive myself to a femoral-stress fracture that could confine me to a plastic boot and sentence me to the pool for months, so I listened to my head when it begged me to exercise patience. I backed off. The leader's pack disappeared in the distance. Knowing that a lot could happen over fourteen miles, I intended to outsmart and catch them in the second half when they tired. For now, I ran alone.

The halfway point appeared out of nowhere. The desiccated Wonderland Lake trail gave way to a rocky mile-long single track that crowned the run's apex and turned us around toward home. I looked up to gage my bearings and saw the shirtless lead pack within striking distance. Just as I had anticipated, they had slowed down considerably from the pace they had set at the onset and had come back to me. Years of experience had taught me what to do next. I lengthened my stride and began to reel in the group. I moved up and quietly latched onto the lead pack, comfortably sliding into their rhythm. We clipped along, two by two, the herd in motion. Our legs glided over the dusty trail as we passed the notoriously fit

Boulder civilians as though they were mere amateurs. This was the moment I had dreamt of, when my Regina teammates picked teams for driveway basketball.

My seven teammates and I reached a fork in the path near the ten-mile mark. Casey, who had been leading, glanced back at the pack. A sophomore, he had started on the team as a "preferred walk-on", someone with varsity capabilities who didn't, however, receive any scholarship money. After two years, the results of his hard work and hitherto untapped talent were obvious. He had recently raced himself onto the varsity team. With potential to contribute to a national championship, he had much to prove.

When Casey spotted me, the only walk-on in the group, he let loose the power in his legs. My teammates looked at one another, their expressions full of inquiry. "What's he doing?" they seemed to ask each other. But everyone knew that Casey planned to crank the pace until I no longer remained with the pack. Maliciously ratcheting up the tempo was an immature move on his part. I knew that in all likelihood, he was motivated by the thought that since he had moved up on the team, he could no longer be seen running with me. I was a perceived threat, not to his spot on varsity, but to his pride.

Like everyone suspected, the pace flew down to about 5:40 minutes per mile. My teammates, wanting to keep it steady, backed off. But I didn't. Casey and I moved ahead and ran shoulder to shoulder. I wanted to let him know that I competed with as much tenacity as any of the varsity runners, including him.

Pitched high in the sky, the unforgiving sun baked the two of us. Between my ribbed torso, concave stomach, and bony shoulders, my long and lean body was built for the heat. I wore my watch, running shoes, and black Nike shorts, now crusted with a chalky line of salt that ran the length of my waistband. It told me I was beyond being dehydrated. Casey, who was also a new roommate at the Fight Club, looked the same. We were four miles, about twenty-five minutes of running, from the field house.

Since Casey had beaten me at the pre-nationals, I deferred the pace-setting duties to him and fell in line with his stride, allowing him to control the speed. According to the team's unwritten rule, the faster man dictated the tempo. Initially, we were not racing—racing in practice was strictly forbidden. Then Casey started to two-step me—that is, run two steps ahead, challenging me to match him. Whenever I threw in a spurt to stay even, he'd react by putting in his own burst. We repeated this again and again. I wanted to tell him to knock it off, to stop *taunting* me.

We hit a rare patch of afternoon shade at the end of Fourth Street. The daylight turned to gloom. Then, without warning, Casey whipped around and glared at me. The tightness in his scrunched red cheeks and the sweat slipping down them told me he wasn't coasting. I could see the wheels in his head spinning. His nose wrinkled. His brow dipped like a gully as he yelled, "McCUE! WHAT THE *HELL* DO YOU THINK YOU'RE DOING? YOU! YOU SHOULDN'T BE *HERE!*"

"Here" came off as a shriek, sounding as if acid had eroded his vocal cords. He charged ahead—one step, two steps, three—without looking back. So did I. Feeling as though a lightning strike had surged through my body, I pulled up next to him, unwilling to accept any more two-stepping. My body had simply reacted. My mind wondered what I had gotten myself into. Granted, our workouts were physically intense, but no one ever yelled at his teammate. Cuss words of every color fired through my mind, but I was just too mad to talk.

Casey and I ran together for another quarter-mile before he pushed ahead to a distance of fifty meters. I was so furious by then that I didn't even try to go with him. I didn't want to run with someone who behaved in that manner. Finishing alone, I realized I had completed one of my fastest training sessions, but for once, it didn't much matter what my watch said. All I could think about was Casey's words echoing in my mind.

I walked into the field house and saw him at the other end, bent over at the waist, stretching his hamstrings. Wetmore was probably in his office. Our teammates would return in a few minutes. I wondered if I should settle the matter with Casey while we were alone. Should I shrug it off and act like it had never happened? Or mention it to Mark? Or ask a teammate for advice?

Emotions in disarray, I kept to myself, chugged my Nalgene, and walked to the ice bath. Soaking my legs in the numbing 38-degree water, I couldn't help but think about the last time I had witnessed someone put his character on the line and violate the code of sportsmanship, which, no matter how desperately anyone wanted to win, had to be upheld. That person was me. What had I been trying to prove, when I threw the second-place medals into the cornfield? Running from the front, I had never looked back to appreciate the effort my Regina teammates were putting in. Judging them by my own definition of victory, I had arrogantly labeled them without a thought for their own perception of success. It had not occurred to me to allow them to choose their own criteria to define it. Now, I knew how it felt. Didn't Casey understand? "Here"—the Buffaloes, Colorado, the miles in the mountains—was all I had. "Here" was my *life*.

The next day, I had no idea how practice would go. I feared being ostracized. As I hesitantly walked to the document, I was met by a bunch of my teammates who apologized for the way Casey had treated me. Grateful for their support, I thanked them and we went about our business as usual. Not wanting to run the risk of Wetmore regarding me as a whiner and a tattle-tale, I kept the matter from him. Still, stories always seemed to have a way of getting back to him. I figured one of my teammates, maybe even Casey, might have told him about what had happened. I hoped for the slightest bit of acknowledgement, nothing quite so definite as an assurance, that I had acted appropriately, but just a "Doing okay?" I would have nodded in assent, even though I was still struggling with, "You shouldn't be *here*." I felt I needed my coach to let my faster teammate know that I was as much a part of the team as anyone else. That never happened. Wetmore, whose utterances were more powerful than I think he realized, never said a word to me. Maybe, he hadn't heard? But what if he had and still hadn't stood up for me?

5. Reconnecting with an old friend: December 2003

One day in December, a month after cross country season was over, I bumped into my old friend Travis. Two months ago, right after the incident with Casey, he had listened to me venting my frustrations, and shared the best advice on how to deal with the situation. He had sounded like Coach Brown. Learn from it, forgive, and then move on, he had counseled me. It was simple stuff. Now on a snowy Monday afternoon, I sought out Travis again. I suggested we run ten miles on the Mesa Trail before admitting that I needed to "take it easy".

"Me too," he replied, grinning.

It had been seven months since Travis had left the team. While we no longer raced, our friendship had endured. We made time to cover the trails that had first connected us. In addition to running, Travis had found other forms of competition, from triathlons to adventure races. He told me how he planned to pace his dad through fifty miles of the Western States 100-mile Endurance Run in the summer. One day, I had flipped through the sports section of *The New York Times* and seen a picture of Travis leading a snowshoe race. Branching out beyond athletics, he now tutored a number of current Colorado athletes at study table, including former teammates who had beaten him.

During his final months on the team, I had wondered if Travis ever asked himself, "Why am I working so hard just to hang in there?" As we crested a ridge, the Colorado campus basking in the sun's alpine glow down in Boulder, I worked up the nerve to ask him the intensely personal question that had been on my mind. "Do you miss it?"

"Nah," he replied, his eyes hidden behind Oakleys, his blond mane cut short.

"Not even a little?" I asked in disbelief.

"I don't think about it like that. Running for Wetmore was awesome, but I've made my decision and moved on, and I think that's actually helped me become a better athlete. I have more balance in my life. I can still run, but I'm glad that I don't have to deal with some other parts of the team anymore."

I prodded further, digging for an explanation. Travis, a 4.0 student, conceded that during his two years on the team, he had constantly reminded himself that he was smarter than nearly everyone else. His admittedly unhealthy way of justifying his self-worth gave him a chance to feel good about himself in a subculture where race times were supposed to define a person.

Wow. His thoughts could have been mine. Strangely, we had never talked about them while we were on the team together. Like Travis, I found that running at Colorado sometimes silently gnawed at me, causing my self-esteem to get lost in the national championship shuffle. Initially, I had thought that constantly comparing myself to my teammates, like Dathan and Jorge, the future Olympians, would serve as an impetus to better myself constantly and force me to rise up. However, I was beginning to realize that the comparisons were having quite the opposite effect. They were dragging me down, demoralizing me. I could have the best race of my life and they would still beat me. It wasn't enough for me to judge my races by what I could accomplish on my own. I had to judge myself against the best. The emotional toll left me feeling inadequate, not just as a runner, but as a person. While my thoughts couldn't destroy my dream, they lingered on the periphery, unwilling to go away. Questions like Travis's had been passing through my head, my heart, and my gut, but I would never give them a voice. Unwilling to acknowledge my innermost fears, I kept them tucked deep inside and focused on the path in front of me.

Running in the crisp Colorado air, surrounded by mountaintops, the endorphins kicking in—it felt like old times as Travis and I skimmed across the trails that were rockier than I had imagined them to be from my porch in Iowa. We descended the frozen tundra, slipping on the coating of fresh snow. At the bottom, my friend finished early so he could go rock climbing or mountain biking or whatever sport his next adventure dictated. Needing a few miles, I kept running.

6. Snow on the trail: February 2004

My eyes flew down the conference championship traveling document, chasing the alphabet. Where was my name? I couldn't find it and its absence didn't make sense. Ten days ago, on a nose hair-freezing February afternoon, I had won my first college race. Sure, it had been a little indoor meet in Lincoln, Nebraska, and only the "B" 3,000 meters at that, but I had thrown up afterwards, spewing the remnants of my lunch—a brown-orange stream of digested bagels, Clif bars, and cookies—all over the parking lot. I had pushed my body so hard that it had revolted! That puke-inducing effort had to count for *something* surely! I felt confident that Wetmore would allow me to enter the next race: the conference championships. While our track schedule listed a complete season, I, along with half of the team, ran from one meet to the next, based partly on my race time and partly on the coach's discretion. If I raced fast enough, he would travel me to the next competition. Since Wetmore had taken me almost everywhere lately, from Eugene, Oregon, to California to Austin, Texas, I looked at the document again and again. My name had to be *somewhere*.

Some students at Colorado lived by their test scores, others according to the ski reports; my life was dictated by the document, the 8.5 by 11-inch piece of white paper that, to the average person, was hardly worth a second look. Wetmore personally wrote the workouts on it in his tight black pen stroke. The traveling document listed the typed names in alphabetical order. It was a given that certain names, like those of my roommates, would always be listed. Tacked to a bulletin board right outside of the coaches' offices, the document was the first place—ahead of teammates, Wetmore, and even the bathroom—that every runner went to before practice. The language on the document was matter-of-fact, unemotional, which was ironic, because it aroused so many feelings within me.

Unable to find "McCue" and make it jump off the page, I finally turned and walked through the crowd of teammates, each busy scanning for his name.

Since the document carried no explanation for my absence, I marched into Wetmore's office in search of one. I found him sitting behind his desk where he seemed much more intimidating than when he'd wander among us, his bulky black fleece tucked into his workout tights. From behind his desk, Mark could play the role of the professor, reminding everyone that even though he had given us book recommendations, there remained a set distance between coach and athlete, him and us. "Matt'er what can I do for you?"

"Mark," I said, my right leg trembling slightly in nervousness, "I checked the list for conference and my name's not on it. I don't understand. What about my race in Lincoln? It was great, remember? I won. Why, then, am I not traveling?"

Wetmore squared up to me. "You'll get your ass kicked. You'll get lapped out of the race."

Nailed between the eyes, I froze. Ass kicked!? I refused to meet the coach's stare and looked instead at the shabby gray carpet, trying to block out his bluntness by not making eye contact. I'd get my ass kicked? Did he really believe that? He had reason to. The year before, I had run the 5k at the indoor conference championships, a race where the Big 12 Conference had an unsettling "lap-out" rule. In simple terms, if someone got lapped on the 200-meter indoor track, which, given Ed's speed, nearly half of the racers would, a white-haired official in a Nebraska Husker-red blazer would wave him off of the track with a plastic red paddle. That had happened to me last year in Lincoln. I had completed two and a half miles and was on personal record pace, when I sensed someone coming up behind me. I started sprinting, but Ed still screamed past. I had never experienced any physical suffering that could be compared to the humiliation of being forced to quit a race by virtue of a plastic paddle. While Coach Brown would have likely found a silver lining in my premature finish, Coach Wetmore stoically directed me outside for a three-mile cool down. I headed into the snowy dark night blinking back tears of frustration, hating myself for working so hard and still not measuring up.

I returned my gaze from the carpet to Wetmore, bit my lip, and muttered, "Okay. Yeah... Thanks." I left the office, unable to stomach another word, my gut hollow.

Practice started in two minutes. My teammates cracked jokes and stretched their calves and quads on the stairs next to the office corridor. I averted my eyes and prayed that none of them had heard the words that may have leaked through Wetmore's open door.

The next weekend, the 2004 Indoor Big 12 Conference Championships came and went without me. As Coach Brown had said, whenever we were struggling over a disappointing race, a crippling injury or, for one of my former teammates, not being named to the homecoming court, "The sun will come up." His wisdom had substance. I wouldn't allow myself to wallow in self-pity for not being named to the traveling list. Instead, I would respond in the only way I knew how. While the rest of the team competed in Lincoln, I decided I would rock a run of epic proportions: the one-two punch of Poorman and Flagstaff Mountain, a challenge so difficult that Mark had never assigned it.

Poorman, a blindingly-steep road that led up one of the unnamed foothills, and the slightly taller 6,690-foot Flagstaff Mountain formed the western edge of Boulder and opened the door to Rocky Mountain National Park rising in the distance. The deep, narrow Boulder Canyon, whose floor was covered by a creek and the busy road, separated Poorman and Flagstaff. Unfortunately, that meant there was no convenient connecting ridge between the two tops. The only way to run both in succession was to lose all of the hard-earned elevation from peaking Poorman and be compelled to gain it back on Flagstaff. Both mountains had well-maintained roads. So most rational people didn't understand why I found it perfectly acceptable to run up them when I could have driven.

Contrary to its humble name, Poorman packed a sharp bite into the mile-long slope that climbed heavenward with reckless abandon. While Flagstaff was the perfect backdrop for a Christmas-card picture, many locals saw the calloused mass of terra firma as a recreational plaything. The hiking trail shot straight up the mountain, just like the pulse of anyone who climbed it. Mileage was irrelevant; the run was a testament of willpower. With my teammates in the heartland, I took solace in Coach Brown's mantra, "It's what you do when no one is looking that matters most." While I wouldn't have him riding alongside me, his wisdom reaffirmed that what I was doing mattered, somewhere, somehow.

Rising early on Saturday morning, I crossed the Fight Club's wooden bridge and started down the sliver that made up the sandy shoulder of the concrete road. The passage remained sketchy even in Boulder County, where drivers were used to roads peppered with runners and cyclists. Around each bend, the full-steam-ahead buses passed within inches of my bony frame. I was immune to the fear of being flattened, but not necessarily because I trusted the drivers who piloted the mammoth rigs. I was just young.

After a mile and a half, I took a left turn at Four Mile Canyon and began charging west and uphill on the skinnier and sketchier Four Mile shoulder. Mid-morning, the smoke gently rose from the chimneys of the log cabins lining the road. I paused, trying to listen to the peaceful sounds of Colorado. All I heard was the air escaping from my lungs and a rushing stream nearby. After a few miles, I hung a sharp right for Poorman Road and began cranking. My quads, calves, lower back, hamstrings, and heart, most of all, instantly felt the sharpness of the incline. I slid into a rhythm and ground out the miles in silence. Breathing techniques be damned! I was just gasping for whatever oxygen I could pull in. I crested Poorman without celebration. It was tough to feel triumphant when I had an even more strenuous mountain ahead.

To reach the base of Flagstaff, I had to run through a quiet residential street. Despite the large number of vegetarian households in

Boulder, the neighborhood I ran past seemed to have the heavenly aroma of bacon wafting from every kitchen.

But I couldn't stop. I had a bigger concern than fried pork, a rarity for me. In my preparation, I had failed to take into account the fact that this was the month of February. Just because I hadn't encountered crusty snow when I peaked Flagstaff in September, it didn't mean the mountain would be clear now. It, of course, wasn't. After summiting, I paused for the briefest of seconds to appreciate the Boulder-valley view, and continued toward the fire road that traversed down the back of Flagstaff Mountain. I hopped over a fence marked "Private", and finished strong on the relatively gentle one-mile tract that led back to the Fight Club. After two hours and ten minutes of sweating, I was home. I was satisfied.

During a weekend when I could have let my frustration cloud my mind, I had adopted an altogether different approach, pushing myself to the outer limits of my endurance. I needed to prove to myself that I still had it, and I passed the test.

The Monday following Big 12's practice began the usual way, with Coach Wetmore walking around the outside of our stretching circle and asking his stock questions. "How are you? Good? How are you? Good?"

Normally, I would have gone about my stretches, but when the coach passed behind me, I couldn't resist turning around and blurting out, "Mark, when you guys were gone, I ran Poorman and Flagstaff."

Having tackled the duo in his younger days, he would know what I was talking about.

"Flagstaff and Poorman, that's a man's run. Congratulations," replied Wetmore, offering his hand.

"It was hard, but worth it," I admitted.

"Good. Then I hope you're ready to go to Stanford. Do you want to?" he casually asked. Sitting next to a few varsity guys, I couldn't believe he was talking to me. Stanford was where Jorge, Ed, and Dathan traveled to race the few collegians faster than themselves. Wetmore was staring directly at me, his eyes probing: Do *you* want to go to Stanford?

Yeah! Of course! Without a doubt! That would be awesome! These were the exclamations that sprang up instantly in my brain.

"Yeah," I said coolly, mirroring Wetmore's impassive expression.

Guys like me who gutted out the twenty-five-lap, 10K distance targeted two key races a year. Taking a crack at more than that would have put too much stress on our legs, left us vulnerable to injuries, and fetched us stale results. The first attempt would come at either Stanford in March or Mount SAC in April. The second would come at our season-ending meet: either the conference or the national championships in May or June. Stanford was a huge and unexpected opportunity. I had no idea what had led Wetmore to take me there. How did it matter? I was going!

"Good," said Mark, "It's in less than a month. Let's get serious." He continued around the circle, asking, "How are you? Good? How are you? Good?" Wetmore both asked and answered his own questions. Once again, he left me wondering what was going through his head.

7. Success by the race clock: March 2004

Daydreaming about Stanford's breathtaking Palm Drive the next day, I continued to focus on achieving success in terms of the race clock. My mother, a high school Religion and Psychology teacher at Regina, knew I had always been wired that way. Despite her best efforts at nurturing, nothing could have changed me. She also knew what I didn't at the time: that success was a word that lent itself to multiple interpretations. Mom would use a simple and straightforward class lesson to have her students define its meaning. She had shared one story with me for "perspective", as she called it. With Stanford on the horizon, my mother's tale had kind of gone in one ear and come out the other. It wouldn't make sense to me until later.

She had her sophomores write down the names of nine successful people. Her only stipulation was that at least one person had to be associated with Regina. Her students used symbols to represent the qualities that made each person worth picking. Michael Jordan would receive a Nike swoosh. A dollar sign would be assigned to Donald Trump. A happy face indicated a non-celebrity. Finally, the students had to whittle their preferred names down to the one person who, according to them, was the most successful of all. One year, my mother had asked her students to read their choices out aloud. Being teenagers, no one raised a hand to volunteer. She had randomly picked a boy to go first.

"Coach Brown," he had said, referring to the man he believed to be a symbol of success.

"Okay, interesting," my mother had conceded, "but why? "Have you been to Coach Brown's house? It's small and it doesn't have a pool. Donald Trump has innumerable houses and pools."

"I know."

"Well have you seen his car?" Mom had persisted. "It's old and rusty. Michael Jordan owns a whole fleet of fast cars."

"I know."

"Then why do you think that Coach Brown is a successful man?"

"Because he's been there for me when I felt no one else was."

"You're not the only one," my mom had replied, nodding. "Who's next?"

This time, the majority of the class raised their hands. My mother picked a girl.

She too said, "Coach Brown."

"Okay, good," replied my mom, "but we've already had him mentioned. So why don't we hear about someone else?"

She looked at her classroom full of runners and football players, band members and honor students, made a sweeping gesture, and asked everyone else to share their influences. She added, jokingly, "If you've picked Coach Brown again, please don't raise your hand."

Not a single hand went up.

VI. WHAT IF MY BEST ISN'T GOOD ENOUGH?

Senior Year

1. What if my best isn't good enough? June 2004

Like I had done in nearly every race thus far, I set a high standard for Stanford. I took my best 10k time, subtracted more than a minute, and set 29:30 as my goal. It shouldn't have surprised me when I missed that unattainable mark. I felt as if the race clock had betrayed me. Or was it that I always set my goals unrealistically high? A few days later, I learned that I was battling anemia again. Great, I thought, not only am I not running fast enough, but my body is also starting to betray me. No matter how many shots of liquid iron I drank, my body never seemed to respond adequately. The rest of my junior season would go steadily downhill, ultimately stagnating in a pool of unfulfilled expectations.

The summer before my senior year, I reflected on my time thus far at Colorado. I had passed on the traditional coming-of-age behavior college students usually displayed, the staple features of which were: partying, skiing, and internships.

No one would fault me for telling Wetmore that I had had a good three years, and now wanted to live like a regular student. I couldn't do that. Before my first Sunday run on Magnolia, I had set myself the goal of contributing to a national championship team. As long as there was another race to run, I would chase my dream.

I poured my hunger into summer base training, preparing for my upcoming year by rising early and covering from ten to twenty miles a day, unabashedly beating up my body. When someone remarked, "One hundred miles a week! Are you crazy!" I'd reply, "That's what it takes," my lips perked up in a faint smile, leaving them to wonder if I was grossly exaggerating or truly insane. I planned to light up the sky or bust. Middle ground just wasn't good enough.

I left Boulder in late June and returned to Iowa for a weeklong visit. With fond memories of "Remember when you were at your best and be there again" ringing in my head, I asked Coach Brown if he wanted to go for a bike ride. Even though I hadn't seen him since Christmas, his reply came without hesitation. He asked me to meet him the next morning at nine, just like the old days.

When we set off, humidity hung heavy in the air, thick and oppressive. My breathing matched the patient rhythm of his pedaling, and, as I looked at Coach Brown to my right, his weathered face never betrayed the effort he was putting forth. The road beckoned in front of us, surging through acres of fields flooded with budding crops. The morning sun shone. As we headed east, the rolling hills gave way to an endless stretch of smooth asphalt. We moved along in a comfortable silence until I began sharing what had haunted me over the past three years.

"I have to make the national championship team," I confided. "I didn't go all the way out to Colorado to be a mediocre fringe runner. There's nothing honorable about merely hanging in there! It's my last chance. I've worked so hard! We have a shot at winning nationals this year. I want to be on that team!"

Coach thought for a moment. "Matt," he finally said, "what have I always told you? Give nothing but your best and the winning will take care of itself."

"Yeah, I know, but that's it! What if my best isn't good enough?" I had finally blurted out the fear, the self-doubt I had kept hidden inside for so long.

What if my best wasn't good enough?

Coach Brown squinted, removed his right hand from the handlebar and reached out. I was running, but he met me with just enough of a squeeze on my skeletal shoulder. He looked directly into my eyes and said, "Your best will be enough."

2. The 2004 Cross Country National Championship: October/November 2004

The Rocky Mountain Shootout, my stepping stone after a summer of tenacious last-chance training, took place in early October. All I could think about was placing in our team's top seven and consolidating my position on the varsity team. To put it in a nutshell, I had had a bad day, and it wasn't the best time to have one. My mid-pack finish wasn't good enough to make the traveling cut for our seven-person national championship roster.

Instead of ending my collegiate cross country career in Terra Haute, Indiana, home to the 2004 NCAA National Championships, I finished it in Fort Hays, competing against schools named after a tomato patch, like Garden City Community College. My self-esteem in grave danger of being blown away in the prairie gusts, I looked to Travis. He had kept his head up on the way to Fort Hays. I vowed to do the same.

Fort Hays State College hosted the five-mile "B" race on its campus right before their homecoming football game. As the homegrown students circled their limestone buildings on hayrack wagons, my opponents and I raced around them. Midway, I ran alone on the edge of the course and followed the white boundary line which wrapped around a small pond next to a dorm. In eighth place, I sprinted to catch the runner in front of me, but I was in no man's land, my closest competitor far ahead and out of sight. I met only wind gusts and a hayrack wagon full of revelers parked off to the side. Under normal circumstances, with my eyes focused on the competition, I wouldn't even have noticed the young man in a trucker hat and a T-shirt cut off at the sleeves among them. But our eyes connected and we held the stare for a fleeting second. As I passed, he yelled, "Run, Forrest, Run!" to the amusement of his friends. Their tumbling laughs rang hollow in my ears. The man held a beer can in his hand like the Statue of Liberty bearing her torch and flashed me a thumbs-up.

A mile later, I closed with a hard-charging kick, passed one guy in the homestretch, and finished in the top ten. Struggling to catch my breath, I tugged at my jersey, now soaked with pools of perspiration. When I tried pulling it over my head, it clung to my body and fought me to stay on. I finally won the contest and began searching for my teammates. Pens of bison that sat on the rim of Fort Hays State's campus blocked my view. A wry smile escaped my lips. Livestock pens and the smell of manure had never appeared in my dreams.

Six weeks later, the outcome in Terra Haute was different. The media experts had named the University of Wisconsin men's team the favorite, but my teammates ran a life-defining race. Wetmore said the guys needed to rise up. Rise up! Everyone did. Colorado won the 2004 National Championship.

Scores of smiling Colorado runners and their parents congregated amid the rural course. The runner's camouflage spikes were caked with muck. Dark, sloshy kickback splattered the backs of jerseys. Everyone was too busy congratulating each other to worry about the impending soaking and scrubbing. A stream of cars from the schools that hadn't earned a first-place trophy drove away from the unpaved parking lot. The only accessible two-lane country road was choked with bumper-to-bumper traffic at a standstill.

As the teams celebrated—the women's team had won too—I stood to the side, huddled in a mud-spattered red ski jacket. My clunky trainers slowly sank into the soft ground where the grass had been uprooted and ripped apart by razor-sharp spikes. It felt like freshman year all over again. Hugs laced with fatigue, heads in the clouds. My teammates were charged with the feeling that life couldn't get any better. The only Colorado runner who had traveled to Terra Haute but hadn't raced, I stood alone, this time without Travis for company in his women's shorts. I tried to feel happy for my teammates, but could feel nothing at all. Numb, I watched the story I had intended to write slip away. For the second time.

3. The hunter and the hunted: December 2004/April 2005

Just as I had done in my freshman year, I drove over to Coach Brown's split-level during Christmas break. I told him about our team, hiding my personal disappointment at being a spectator. Aware that I hadn't run, Coach made it a point to repeat something I had heard him say long ago: "Remember that everyone on the team is important, because without the guys in the back, there would be no one to push the team forward."

When it was time to leave, I parted with a tired "Merry Christmas". My thoughts were on returning to Colorado and tying up loose ends. As long as I had another race to run, my dream—forced to evolve beyond a national championship—would remain alive. One semester of school and an entire track season in hand gave me enough time to finish my Colorado run successfully. What would define success? To race unbelievably fast, I decided. I had done it before, in my final season of high school track. That very thought inspired me with the confidence that would follow me through late March into April and springtime, a season for new beginnings. In six weeks, the quest I had pursued so single-mindedly would be over, a prospect I wasn't ready to consider as of yet.

One Saturday morning, I let my mind ramble on my way to clicking off an easy ten-miler. My final Mount SAC Relays was in three weeks. A crisp, cool night under the California stars was the perfect place to cash in all of my searing sessions on Magnolia. With over eighty collegians entered in the 10,000 meters, my race guaranteed nothing but sheer madness. But I was fit—and hungry.

Freshly showered, I pulled up to the Fight Club's granite kitchen counter, unfolded the sports section, and sat down to my favorite breakfast: homemade peanut butter granola doused with fresh cream. After I had picked up my spoon, the phone rang. On the other end, my mother began, "Matt, are you sitting down?"

"Who's dead?" I blurted out, thinking immediately of my grandparents. The knot in my throat loosened when Mom told me in a distracted, timid voice that no one had died.

Then, as I took a large bite of granola, I heard her say, "It's Coach Brown." Her words seemed to emerge with difficulty, offering details that were far more painful than knock-out punches: pancreatic cancer—Stage Three—inoperable.

Oh...my...God...

I stood up, unable to swallow another bite. In the living room, my roommates lounged on the leather couches and slurped cereal in front of the TV, oblivious to the news I had just received. The familiar SportsCenter theme music played. Highlights began. It was like every other Saturday morning at the Fight Club. Except for the words my mother had uttered. They were loaded enough to shatter glass.

Leaving the dim kitchen, I climbed the stairs to my room, my ear glued to the phone. I had barely closed the door when my face flushed with pent-up emotion. An insatiable hunger gnawed at my belly, as if I hadn't eaten in days. I felt the edge of my bed, ready to support my quaking body. But I couldn't sit down. I paced, gnawed on my fingernails, and, like a trial lawyer, tried to talk my mother out of her horrible news. There was little to say, so much to ask. I needed—was desperate for—some space. The news had hit me from nowhere. It was too much to handle, the weight of it unbearable.

Calling from Iowa, my mom said that Coach Brown had pulled her aside, earlier in the morning, before Regina's track meet. According to her, he had been feeling "crummy" for a month and had finally decided to visit his doctor. He had been given a week's worth of tests. The day before—April Fool's Day—he had been diagnosed.

"Very few people know about it at this point," Mom said. "None of his athletes know, and he's not going to tell them until after today's meet. Coach Brown said he didn't want his boys worried about him when they had races to run."

I had had no idea of how grave things were with Coach. Focused on my last season, I hadn't talked to him since I wished him a Merry Christmas.

"He's going in for a second opinion next week," my mother's voice continued, "but the results of the initial tests were pretty conclusive."

Shock was turning into reality when I asked, "Mom, how bad is it really? Will I ever see him again?" The words "inoperable" and "cancer" scared me, but what did they actually mean?

When my mother replied, "All of Coach Brown's children and grandchildren are coming home immediately," the severity of his illness sank in. Two of Coach's daughters lived in Guam, a world away.

Alone in Colorado, more than 800 miles from home, I was left to grapple with my feelings alone. There was no one here I could wrap my arms around for comfort; nor was there someone who would do the same to me to ease my pain.

After I had hung up, my first thoughts were of the boys competing for Regina. How would they take the news? Later that day, after Regina's meet, I called my younger brother Patrick, a junior on the team. Listening to him, I realized that even though miles and years separated me from Coach Brown's current boys, the news had deeply affected us all. It united everyone not by the championships we had won, but by our love for one man, the cornerstone of our tradition.

Patrick related how after the home meet, Coach had gathered the boys' team in the middle of Regina's track—the same track that would, one day, be named after him. He had remained standing as his boys sat around him. Regina had won the meet. So he had spent a long time handing out the medals to the individual victors and relay teams. Then he had done what he always did: he had said a little something about every other athlete who had given his best effort, regardless of whether he had won a medal. But before the boys could disperse and walk away, Coach Brown had asked them to move in closer. The subtle, but unmistakable inflexion in his calm voice hinted that something wasn't quite right. The boys had fallen silent, wondering what was coming. Then Coach Brown had begun, "I haven't been feeling very good lately. So, I went to the doctor last week, and they ran some tests. They discovered I have pancreatic cancer. That's not a good one to have, and I may not be able to make it to practice every day from here on out, but I plan to coach the rest of the season."

The news had been slow to hit. This was the last thing the boys had expected to hear. A few of them had picked up their track spikes, walked to their cars, and driven out of the Regina parking lot, unsure of how to behave when the man they loved had shared such devastating news with them. The boys weren't aware of pancreatic cancer's cruelty, but the shrill word alone—*cancer*—was enough to crush them.

With tears welling up in their eyes, the rest of the team had picked their physically-drained bodies off the black surface and formed a single-file line in front of Coach Brown. No one had told them to do it; the line was of their own making. On the empty high jump pit in the middle of the deserted track, each boy had taken his turn to wrap his arms around their resilient coach. Some had looked him straight in the eye when they embraced him. Others had buried their face in his shoulder. Either way, none could hold back their tears.

4. April Fools: April 2005

According to my family, Coach Brown's diagnosis ignited a firestorm in our Iowa town. Those whose hearts he had touched, like the classroom of Regina students who had picked him as the most successful person in the world, were crippled with grief, frustration stemming from helplessness, and unanswered questions. It was a test of faith and a stream of tears. No one knew how to react. What would be the right thing to do? Pray? Send a card? Bake cookies? As people often did, they looked to Coach Brown for direction. When the local paper ran an article on his diagnosis, Coach said, "I've always been the kind of person that feels that all people, not only kids, need to get and give hugs. I've gotten a lot of hugs lately…"

That's how people responded. Brown's fight against inoperable cancer had begun with an outpouring of hugs.

The following week, when people weren't around to embrace, like in the darkness of midnight when an exhausted Coach Brown found himself unable to sleep, loneliness would creep up on him. He later admitted to me that it was the moment his sadness would turn to anger and aggression over the cruel blow fate had dealt him. The questions would crowd around him: why had he initially gone to the doctor, assuming he had allergies, only to return for a CAT scan? Why had he, of all people, been the patient, when the doctor began, "I wish I could tell you it was just an allergic reaction"? Why was his cancerous mass wrapped around two major veins, making surgery all but impossible? Why did he have to get saddled with the disease that the Johns Hopkins' medical website called "the challenge of the twenty-first century"? He was a good man. Why did it have to happen to him?

Privately, he had confessed to one of his daughters, home from Guam, "I don't want to die."

She had looked him in the eye and replied, "Dad, don't think, 'I don't want to die.' Think, 'I want to live.'"

His daughter's words resonated within him. He would never let the kids he coached feel sorry for themselves. What good reason did he have to do so? The more he thought about it, the more he realized he didn't have anything to regret. He had a loving family. He had a mother who would relentlessly pray for him. He had received more baked goods in the past week than he could possibly eat. His wife Darlene had already been diagnosed with breast cancer twice and had beaten it both times. In the small-town community of Iowa City and Regina, Coach Brown had an army of supporters, some of whom he knew and others that he didn't, like the elderly woman who had approached him one Sunday morning after Mass and said, "You don't know who I am, but I know who you are and I'm praying for you."

On April Fool's Day, 2005, Coach Brown's life changed. The sixty-two-year-old father of four began a new life: "AC" or "after cancer", as he referred to it. The man who had pulled the positive from every rough situation, even found something to be grateful for in his Stage Three inoperable diagnosis: he didn't have Stage Four. Death.

"I want to live," would, from then on, become his motto.

5. What if your best isn't good enough? April 2005

I called Coach Brown the day after I had heard the news about his cancer. Four unanswered rings led directly to his machine. After the prompt, I had an open-ended forum to say whatever I wanted, needed, to tell him. I planned to start by saying I was sorry that he had pancreatic cancer. To not worry; he would beat it. That I would do whatever I could, whatever he needed. That he couldn't die—I wouldn't let him. None of those words ever left my mouth. Instead, I hung up halfway through my message, because my voice cracked, and I couldn't hold back the tears that ran uncontrolled down my cheeks.

I called again the next day.

Coach answered with a somber "Hello" on the first ring. When I told him who it was, he said, "*Matt* McCue, what's new with you?"

I wanted to vent, because my hip had felt a little sore after my morning run. Then I had got home and realized I didn't have any skimmed milk for my peanut butter granola. So I had had to use powdered milk, which tasted like chalk. I couldn't possibly complain about such inconsequential things to Coach Brown. Suddenly, life had acquired a whole new meaning that would force my perspective to evolve and mature.

He and I broke through the small talk about the weather and got to the part where he admitted, "Matt, you know that, statistically, I have the worst kind of cancer people can get."

He was right. The numbers said he would be dead in nine months. But Coach said he wasn't ready to become a statistic. He was ready to beat cancer.

"How?" I asked.

"I'm going to take it one day at a time and give nothing but my best."

"But what if giving your best isn't good enough!" I interjected, sharing the thought that frightened me the most, "You'll die! Aren't you scared your best might not be enough this time?"

"Matt," he began, his words patiently flowing into my ear as if he were right beside me, sharing the secret to life, "I'm going to do the best that I can, but ultimately, it's up to Him."

6. In the glimmer of national championship trophies: April 2005

At the Fight Club two weeks later, I placed the last of my Nike gear into my black duffel as I prepared to leave for the Mount SAC Relays. Before I toggled my spike bag, I walked to the bookshelf and found my wooden picture box tucked behind a row of books. *Running with the Buffaloes* was in tatters, falling apart from overuse. I flipped through my photos, including the ones of my Colorado team celebrating victories, and stopped at the shot of the Drake Relay's 3,200 meters. It looked exactly as I remembered it—Coach Brown and me. I picked it up. My movements were spontaneous, instinctive. I can't explain my motivation. Packing the high school picture felt like such an insignificant, silly act in the glimmer of the national championship trophies on display throughout the house. What did that matter now? I gently placed the print inside my gym bag. All I could think about was ear-splitting country music, the kind Coach had once played.

7.   The 2005 Mount SAC Relays 10k. *Part 2:* April 2005

"How about that!" I said to my parents, two of the very few spectators left in the thinning Mount SAC stands. It was almost eleven p.m., but my endorphins had kicked in. I was ready to celebrate my incredible 10,000-meter race with In-N-Out.

"There's a chance you ran one lap short," my parents replied, wincing before the final word left their mouths. My mother's stopwatch remained wrapped around her neck. Her right hand gripped the buttons. My brother and sister hovered behind them. They didn't refute our parents.

"What!" I exclaimed. "What are you talking about? No…that can't be true! It can't be! I ran the race—all twenty-five laps! I had the lap count in my head! Every time I ran past the starting line, the official yelled the same number I had. Another official told me when I had one to go! A third directed me off the track at the finish! If I ran one lap short, why didn't someone catch me or tell me or…something!"

"We never said you did it on purpose. With the sixty or seventy or however many participants in the race, you probably lost track of the lap count and the officials miscounted. We don't know for sure."

"But I ran so fast!"

"Go talk to Wetmore," they suggested. "He'll help you sort it out."

This couldn't be happening.

I found Mark seated fifteen rows up in the bleachers, wrapped in his black Colorado jacket, his burlap satchel on his lap. He wore his stocking cap like a midshipman, right above the ears. I sidled up next to him, thinking my parents couldn't be right. Please tell me it can't be right, I said silently.

Coach Wetmore spoke first. "Matt'er, you cut your race one lap short."

"No… Are you sure?" Please say no.

"Yes, by my count—"

"But three separate officials told me the same thing. Finish!" I theatrically gestured, hoping that would make a difference.

"I don't know what to tell you. You ran one lap short," Wetmore reiterated with a shrug.

"But…but…"

And that was that.

I thought my time, 29:33 for 6.2 miles, or 4:45 per mile had seemed fast. However, Mount SAC represented the essence of distance races. The best collegiate distance runners in the nation traveled here to run unbelievably fast times. A million thoughts had consumed my mind during the race of endless circles. Apparently, an accurate lap count wasn't one of them.

Coach Wetmore and I sat in silence and looked across the desolate track. At what, I don't know. The dirt-red oval was bare. The day's races had finished. Mark finally told me to head out for a cool-down. He said that was what I needed.

I walked away from the electric stadium lights toward the grass warm-up field that sat alone on the far side of the track. Sprawling on the hard cold ground, I let my soaked jersey cling to my dry chest and shivered. When I opened my gym bag in search of a clean shirt, I found the Drake Relays picture. Once crisp, it was now slightly crumpled. But while the edges were bent, the image remained clear. Coach Brown's arms were still thrust skyward for me, his support unwavering. The picture was a testament to our relationship: Coach standing in the background and caring for me in a way that I had never noticed, because I was young and restless and focused solely on the ground ahead of me. What I would have given for a hug from him right now.

I gently placed the picture back in my bag and stared at the lifeless grass plot. I wanted to bury my emotions: the discontent in my heart and the confusion in my head. The harder I tried to cast them away, the more intense they became, crowding the moment with pain and anger and frustration. The night was supposed to define my time at Colorado as a success. It couldn't have been any worse. I had only one solution.

Run. Hard.

I left the stadium. The street lamps lit the way. The clock left little room before midnight. For the first time in my life, I started a run without clicking my watch. I took off down some nameless street and sprinted into the night.

8.   Final chance: April 2005

I arrived at practice the following week and proceeded to the document. Wetmore had listed my name for the day's workout. That told me I had more races left to run. I had expected to feel relieved, but my relief was overshadowed by a lingering embarrassment. I had trouble explaining the "lap count" debacle to my teammates. I had no answers, just the same subdued refrain, "I don't know." I was still trying to figure it out myself. I showed up to practice, ran hard on the hard days, easy on the easy days, and sought the one person who would understand: Travis.

"Want to go for a run on the Mesa?" I asked him one day, when we didn't have team practice. This time, I shared the thoughts I had once suppressed, comforted, because I had an ally in Travis, whether I ran fast, slow or one lap short.

Two weeks after the Mount SAC Relays, Wetmore posted the outdoor conference championship's traveling document. To earn a coveted seat on the bus to Kansas State University, we had to have one of following:

1. Be in the top ten on the Big 12 Lists
2. Finished in the top eight at a previous Big 12 championship meet
3. Senior

Senior? That wasn't an accomplishment. I had become a senior merely by hanging in there. I didn't argue. I had one final opportunity to redeem myself.

9. Nothing but my best: May 2005

The crimson track at Kansas State University in Manhattan, Kansas shoulders the campus. A backdrop for the mammoth football field, it could have been mistaken for almost any track in America. On Sunday afternoon, the final day of the meet, I prepped for the start of the 5,000 meters by easing into a final warm-up stride and rising to full speed, gliding across the track before slowly decelerating to a stop. My stone-faced competitors were scattered around me, lost in their own thoughts, unwilling to make eye contact, lest they lose their killer instinct. In the bleachers, I spotted my parents and younger brother Tim. Between them, they had barely missed a race of mine. I couldn't have asked for a better support system.

The moment begged for nostalgia, but I couldn't look back on the past ten years. Doing so would have confused the butterflies in my stomach. I needed them flying in the right direction. Forward.

For the first time in my life, I had a goal more honorable than winning. I wanted to blast each of the twelve and a half laps, as if I would never be allowed to run again. I succeeded, finishing twenty-eighth out of fifty-eight runners.

The cicadas buzzed incessantly and the gentle breeze tugged at the muggy air as my eight teammates and I walked off the track in the direction of Wetmore, standing alone on the backstretch. Mark stopped our top guy and said a few words to him about his win. Then he spoke to another about his third-place finish. Wetmore caught me trailing the rest. "Matt'er, last race in a Buffalo uniform," he said, locking his eyes on me and tilting his head, giving what I interpreted as a nod of respect for hanging in there. Though the interaction lasted no more than 10 seconds, it was one of the best compliments anyone had ever paid me.

Hours later, our chartered bus roared over the Kansas plains. I called Coach Brown. "How was your race?" he asked. He knew it was my last.

I glazed over my finish time and told him I had given nothing but my best, and that had been enough.

When he replied, "I always knew you had it in you," I could tell he was smiling.

10. Res severa verum gaudia: May 2005

Two days later, I walked into Wetmore's office and found him behind his desk. I carried my final letter for him. It had a simple theme: "Thank you for giving a young dreamer from Iowa a chance."

"You've been a loyal, hardworking, and dedicated member of the team, all the characteristics we look for in a Buffalo," he said. "What do you have planned next?"

"I'm heading back to Iowa for a little bit. I have a few people I need to see. Then I'm off to New York City to find work as a journalist. Six months ago, I thought that making it in New York would be too hard. Impossible. Then I told myself, 'If you think you can or you think you can't, you're right.' I have to try."

"Do you have a job?"

"No…I've applied to something like seventy-five publications, any place that employs writers. I haven't heard back from one. Whatever. New York is the land of opportunity. I know I don't have anything there—no friends, nowhere to live. I'm going to give nothing but my best and the rest will take care of itself."

Each time I shared my future plans, my aspirations sounded crazier. I could only imagine what Wetmore would say.

"Don't give up," he said, "Of all the coaches who began when I did ten years ago, not many of them are still around today. For one reason or another, they've moved on from running."

Fond of literature himself, the coach told me about many unknown writers who had moved to New York City and survived in overcrowded apartments, devoid of plumbing or electricity, and endured hunger and loneliness as they went about crafting their stories. I preferred not to go an entire year without a working toilet, but I appreciated Wetmore's words of wisdom.

Five minutes passed, and the coach picked up his pen. I stood, reached across his desk, with the half-written workout upon it, and firmly shook his hand. With three national championships in four years, the University of Colorado team and Coach Wetmore were more compelling than ever. With no regrets, I walked out, smiling at the words floating across his computer screen: "*Res severa verum gaudia.*"

To be serious is the greatest joy.

11. Now I know: May 2005

When I landed in Boulder, a green eighteen-year-old who had lost his way on his very first day there, I had fallen in love with Colorado. I had vowed to stay there forever. But now, I was leaving town in the early morning darkness, resisting the impulse to sneak one final peek in my rearview mirror and watch the Flatirons fade away. Twenty-two years old, I had lived my dream. I had run with the Buffaloes. It was time to move on. My journey had been humbling and invigorating. When I began, I had run with abandon, like an unbroken colt, unwilling to be part of the stable. Leaving for Colorado was my opportunity to run with the herd, the most dominant in the land. I had arrived in Boulder with little but the value of hard work ingrained in my mind and a vision clouded by idealism.

I deemed my Colorado run a success. I had given "nothing but my best"; that was how I had grown to define the term. While I had expected to leave college with national-championship rings and All-American certificates, I drove away with lessons learned and wisdom gained. I could say, "Now I know."

Mesmerized by the bright lights of the greatest city in the world, I realized my next journey would be similar to my first. I would be pursuing my new goal of becoming an author, an aspiration my mother realistically judged far more challenging than walking on with the Buffaloes. I planned to arrive in New York like many college graduates, with the clothes on my back and an intoxicating dream in my head. Hadn't I learned anything?

I had. I had experience on my side, a newfound maturity on my shoulders, and support from home, no matter what happened in Manhattan. I would take Coach Brown's quotes—the ones I had always assumed were meant to make me run faster—and use them where he had intended me to do so. In life.

The night before I left Boulder, I spoke to my mother on the phone, asking her "Does any of the running stuff I've done matter?"

There was a pause before she replied, "It mattered to you."

She was right. Looking back, I decided it wasn't the 100-mile weeks, Magnolia Road or the allure of a championship that really mattered. What was important was a coach in Iowa who had always cared for me even when I ran away from him. It was my turn to wrap my arms around him. I headed home to stand by his side.

12. Blue on your shoes: May 2005

After ten hours of driving east, I took a detour through Des Moines and walked into Drake Stadium, home to the 2005 Iowa Boys' Track and Field State Championships. Instinctively, I ducked under the stands, walked into the light, and saw the blue track crowded with athletes warming up in frayed uniforms. Even though watches beeped every time the gun cracked, it was as if time had stood still during the past four years.

I could see him from a distance. Surrounded by assistant coaches, he looked frail, but instantly recognizable. He was taking a catnap, his head tilted to the left, the sparse salt-and-pepper hair poking out from underneath his navy blue ball cap. I walked over and lightly tapped him on the shoulder. Startled, he turned around. When he saw who it was, he stood up and gathered me in his arms. Flashing a grin, Coach Brown began, *"Matt* McCue, I'm glad to see you here..."

13. Legend of the Fall: November 2007 The final entry

One story ends and in its wake, another begins. Bob Brown's supporters in Iowa and those spread throughout the country, the people who wore purple bracelets specifically in support of those suffering from pancreatic cancer, knew that Coach had begun the fight for his life on April Fool's Day 2005. He had immediately started chemo and, over the next year, had lost forty pounds as a result. However, he retained two weighty tools: his ability to give a crushing hug and his faith. His supporters hoped and prayed for the Miracle Cure.

Even after the most upsetting race results, Coach Brown had been able to fall back on his ability to extract the positive elements from the day's events. In a similar vein, his diagnosis spurred people into acknowledging how much he meant to them. To hold the steady flow of get-well cards, Darlene bought a thick plastic binder. It quickly filled. Then it overflowed. Coach would end up needing seven binders to house the abundance of letters that filled his mailbox for months. Every day, for the next two and a half years, a different person would tell him how much they loved him. During the summer after graduation from Colorado, I spent many humid afternoons at Coach Brown's house, sitting on his shaded back porch and simply listening to his stories. One day, I casually mentioned that I was writing a book about the two of us. He smiled and, seemingly at a loss for words, left it at that, humbled, I think, by my intentions. To Coach Brown, it had never been about him. It had always been about his athletes.

Despite the circumstances, we knew that life had to go on. In early August 2005, I wrapped him in a monster hug and told him goodbye. As I drove away, I wondered if I would ever see Coach again. Thankfully, I would.

Once I arrived in New York City, I had nowhere to live. Nor did I have a job waiting. And neither friends nor a mentor like my old coach were around to fall back on. Opening the cab door and setting foot in Manhattan, I thought: *This is for real. No turning back.* I was officially a stranger in a strange land. In addition to Coach

Brown's quotes, all I carried with me were two suitcases and the understanding that New York was the right place for a dreamer like me.

My first few months were as brutal as they were exhilarating. Brown's grandfathered maxim, "If you think you can or you think you can't, you're right," sustained me as I settled in. There was no way I could utter, "I can't," when he himself, challenged by a much taller order, was repeating to himself every moment, "I can. I can. I can." Unable to land a "real" job, I took an unpaid editorial internship at *Rolling Stone*. After work, I would tutor a sixth-grade boy, earning $40 a night. It was barely enough to scrape by. The multiple-job workdays left me little time to work on my story. So I borrowed a page from my Regina cross country early-morning-practice days and started waking at five, rising and running in the darkness that veiled Central Park, and then writing before I went to work. As I finished Coach Brown's story and mine, I couldn't help but wonder: how would his version end?

In June 2006, a little more than a year after Coach's diagnosis, the Miracle Cure presented itself. In short, the cancer had separated from one of the major veins to which it had been attached. He could now undergo the intricate fourteen-hour surgery required to remove the mass. During the daylong operation, students and parents filled Regina's chapel to "storm heaven" by quietly praying together. Late that night, word spread that Coach Brown had almost died a couple of times on the operating table, but despite a substantial loss of blood, he had made it. He would live. The only source of anxiety was the few fugitive cancer cells that might have gotten away and were on the loose inside his body. A few days later, the tests came back negative. The margins were clear. Cancer free! The Miracle Cure! Coach Brown, the hero! Our small, tight-knit community could now heave a sigh of relief, something we hadn't been able to do for the past year.

Again, the cards poured in. This time, I tried to arrange for one person in particular to send his best wishes. After months of discussion with a nice woman at his foundation, I received word that this hero was sending Coach Brown a congratulatory note. A few days later, Coach found the very encouraging handwritten letter from Lance Armstrong in his mailbox. He described it as "neat".

Unfortunately, the cancer-free road turned rocky a year later in June 2007. Brown visited the hospital for some follow-up tests and found out that his markers were acting up. The cancer had returned—a survivor's worst nightmare. Coach Brown didn't carry any extra weight; yet, more flesh seemed to melt away from his body to the point where his cheeks sank so far back into his face that it looked like he had nothing at all beneath the taut skin covering his facial bones. Doctors claimed he was the most seriously ill pancreatic-cancer patient they had ever witnessed. None had apparently survived till this crippling stage. It was a struggle to finish my story while, tucked away in the back of my mind, I knew he was slowly and painfully dying. I had many one-sided conversations with God, during which I lit into him for Coach Brown's plight, one that seemed grossly undeserved.

August 2007. My close circle of prized editors—my mother who had all four of her children compete for Bob Brown, my younger brother Patrick, and my writing mentor Iowan Dave Gould, a filmmaker and father of two children who had run for the Coach—told me that I needed to send him a copy of the manuscript soon—very soon. Sensing their urgency, I did. Though every word in it wasn't set, the focus was crystal clear: a coach had changed my life. Coach Brown would be an inspiration, the man who had used the values learned in long distance running to beat death.

But that would never come to pass.

Fast forward to October 2007. The raging toxins had nearly seized Coach' entire body, and, by all accounts from his doctors, he certainly shouldn't have been alive at this point. But he was holding on, because one of his daughters was getting married and he wanted to be by her side on that special occasion. I truly believe that though Coach Brown's body had given up, he had willed himself to make it to the wedding day, so that he could walk his daughter down the aisle. Before the ceremony, she confided to him—and him alone—that she was pregnant with a male child. She would proudly name her son Robert.

After the wedding was over, it would only be a matter of time. Coach felt he was slipping and quietly let a few others know. He had taped a note on his refrigerator. It bore a quote whose message he had never conveyed to his runners: "Let God let go."

My mentor was readying himself for death.

The past two and a half years had given me plenty of time to make my peace. I had written and called and stopped by his house, never missing a chance to say hello. That didn't make the end any easier. I would always desire one more crushingly tight hug. I knew the last words I ever uttered to Coach Brown had said it all. "No matter what happens," I had told him a week before he died, "know that I love you."

As for the story, I set a deadline for the manuscript's completion. After more than two years, I picked a random day in a random week: Tuesday, November 6, 2007. On that date, buoyed by a sense of satisfaction, I sent finished drafts to my mother, brother, and Dave.

Later that week, on a Sunday morning, my mother called and, speaking in a grave voice, left an unusually abrupt message: "Matt, call me."

That's when I knew. I was walking home from church. It was a sunny, but cold day in New York City and the cloudless blue sky offered a clear path to heaven. I knew Coach Brown was now resting comfortably there, thankfully watching over me.

Four days later, the number of people who showed up for his funeral proved to be a testament to the place this man had managed to make for himself in our hearts. By nine-thirty a.m., there was standing room only at the 800-person-capacity St. Mary's Catholic Church. The service was scheduled to start at ten. The number of people who had turned up was an awe-inspiring sight considering that Regina High School had about 250 students and the large majority of them *weren't* runners. For the entire Mass, I gritted my teeth and stared straight ahead at the whitewashed wall behind the altar. I didn't dare let my gaze fall on the casket, and I knew that if I caught the eye of those around me who couldn't hold back their tears, I would fall apart.

At the graveyard, the wind blew violently, the gray clouds hung low, and light flurries tapped the ground—it was Regal weather, the kind of crummy day on which Coach Brown's runners always managed to rise above. It made everyone pause and smile and remark that Coach had had a hand in the conditions. As the crowds left the cemetery, a number of former Regina runners whom I hadn't seen in years asked if I had written a story about our teacher.

"Yeah," I replied, "how'd you know?"

"Coach told us," they said, adding, "he was very proud of it, and of you."

Jesus. That did it. I completely broke down. The words twisted my insides, ripped my throat, and filled my eyes with tears—of sadness for that day, and of joy for the future, when life would begin anew and I could carry on, with hopes of becoming a "Coach Brown" in the life of a passionate young man, someday.

ACKNOWLEDGEMENTS

Writing a book can feel like the loneliest experience in the world. However, as I typed this section, I realized that there were far more people involved in the story than I had ever anticipated. It gives me great joy to be able to say the following.

This story wouldn't have been possible without Coach Brown and Coach Wetmore, two towering figures in my life. What more can I say in appreciation that I haven't already?

Chad Swope, Super Dave, and Jay Johnson, all behind-the-scenes assistant coaches, were quiet heroes who mentored me, along with many others, through the simple act of running.

Thanks to my Iowa friends, Jimmy and Matthew Larew, Meghan Hargrave, Katey Dorweiler, Chris Hale, Steve Sherwood, Eric Ratliff, and the Dwyer's.

I was fortunate to compete with a number of great guys over the years including Justin Kron, Tony Bothell, and David Welsh at Regina and Erik Heinonen, Travis Macy, and Jorge and Ed at Colorado.

A special thanks to the King family, the Cheley family, and Mark Tex Tuggle.

Thank you to those who I've met in New York: Geoff and Erin, Hilary and William, Kate, Louise, Katherine, Catherine, and Carly Gresh. To Doug, Sarah, and Elizabeth, for listening to me constantly talk about this story.

Thank you to those who shared their time with a young aspiring writer like me: Mike Sager, Jim Ryun, Bill Rodgers, David Margolick, John and Donna Dye, Peter Gambaccini, Toby Tanser, David Friend, Doug Stumpf, Renee Lewin, and Liz Smith.

Dave Gould, you changed my life, guiding me with the patience of a man who had been there before. I desperately needed a mentor during this process, and you were it.

Where would I be without my family?

To Nanny and Papa. Thank you for always asking about my story during our weekly phone calls. Your belief in me was unwavering, your wisdom plentiful.

To Tim. Thanks for once commandeering a golf cart during a cross country races so you could cheer me on. You almost got arrested, but I'd say it was worth it.

To Patrick. Thanks for your brutal honesty with my writing, and creative flair for design and language. Your prints are all over this story.

To Sarah. Thanks for your patience in giving up the social scene at the Regina Fun Festival every Labor Day weekend, just to come to Boulder and watch me run.

To mom. Thanks for riding your bike alongside your then 12-year-old son on those early, bitterly cold January mornings long ago. Without your headlight leading the way, I would have surely been hit by a car.

To dad. Thanks for coming to all of my races, especially the one in Fort Hays where I felt like the world was going to end. Also, thanks for buying me In-N-Out out in California.

Coach Brown taught me to always be sure to hold family close and never lose an opportunity to tell them how much I love and appreciate them. Thankfully, I do.

Coach and athlete, teacher and student...whatever the
term that defined our relationship, this picture just brings
a smile to my face.